UNSTUCK

1/19/16

Bill,

   All my best to you
and your business
coaching !

Your friend,
Jon

JON DENNEY

UNSTUCK

13 business strategies along with specific action steps to help serious business owners earn more money, have more time, and significantly increase company value.

Because without action, nothing happens!

TATE PUBLISHING
AND ENTERPRISES, LLC

Published by Tate Publishing & Enterprises, LLC
127 E. Trade Center Terrace | Mustang, Oklahoma 73064 USA
1.888.361.9473 | www.tatepublishing.com

Tate Publishing is committed to excellence in the publishing industry. The company reflects the philosophy established by the founders, based on Psalm 68:11,
"The Lord gave the word and great was the company of those who published it."

Book design copyright © 2014 by Tate Publishing, LLC. All rights reserved.
Cover design by Rtor Maghuyop
Interior design by Jake Muelle

Published in the United States of America

ISBN: 978-1-63268-447-9
Business & Economics / Development
14.08.01

INTRODUCTION

Business owners tend to occasionally get stuck in their businesses. If you're a business owner, you know what I'm talking about.

After years of steady growth, your sales revenue seems to have plateaued, and you can't figure out why. You're stuck.

Or maybe your sales are increasing, but your profitability is not. No matter how hard you try, you just can't seem to reach your profit goals. You're stuck.

Other common areas of "stuck-ness" include lack of cash, people issues, service failures, quality issues, recurring problems that never seem to go away, company culture issues, and an overall lack of leadership depth.

Or maybe you just feel like you are stuck. You did a wonderful job of starting your company or in taking the reins of an existing company. You knew exactly what needed to be done and you got it done. But now, you're unsure.

You ask yourself:

- What is a business owner supposed to do once the "start-up" phase is over?

- How do I get my business to finally start throwing off cash?

- How do I free myself up to be able have more balance in my life?

- How can I build a stronger team so I don't have to be so involved in everything?

- How can I get this business to run without me?

- How can I dramatically increase the value of my company?

- How can I make my company more attractive to potential buyers?

- What do other successful business owners do with their time?

Here's a fact: The successful strategies that helped you build your business to where it is today were great strategies to get you here, but they are not the same strategies required to get you or your business to the next level. Simply stated, your business is stuck because you're using stale strategies that no longer work!

The great news is, there's a lot you can do about it, and none of it is particularly difficult although it does require attention and action.

This book is intended to get business owners refocused on the business fundamentals required to take your business to the next level. Some of it may be refresher training, some of it will include old concepts put in a way that gives you a new understanding, and some of it will be brand-new to you. Whatever the case may be, one thing is certain: you will absolutely begin the process of getting yourself and your company unstuck if you put these fundamentals into action.

Books are a great way to get smarter, and we all know the old adage: Knowledge is power. But I think that's one of the biggest lies of all time! Knowledge in and of itself is worthless until that knowledge is applied through action. So when I wrote this book, I had that in mind.

Unstuck contains a series of strategies centered on building, growing, and maximizing the benefits of business ownership. But it doesn't stop there! After each strategy, there are a series of smart and specific action steps you can take in your business to immediately put these strategies into action and get the results you're looking for.

At the end of the book, I added a chapter on the not-so-smartest things I've done as a business owner and some things I've seen others try that didn't work out so well for them. Maybe you've made some of these mistakes yourself. Or maybe reading about them will help you avoid making these mistakes in your own business. It's always less expensive to learn from someone else's mistakes. Well, here's your opportunity!

This book is chock-full of "golden nuggets." Even applying a single action step in only one strategy could make a significantly favorable impact on your company's profitability and value. If you commit to taking smart action on several of the strategies discussed, the results can be truly amazing.

Please go ahead and turn to the Table of Contents to get a flavor for what's in store for you in this book. Then, pick the topic that can help you most right now and start there. This book was written so that you can read the white papers in any order you wish. So please start with the area you're most stuck and move on from there. But by all means, don't move on to the next strategy until you first take action!

After all, action is power; knowledge is just a good start. So get after it and get unstuck. You can do this!

-Jon

CONTENTS

Introduction 5

Strategy 1: My Company Owns Me. 21

This is for people who feel like their businesses own them instead of the other way around. If you feel like you don't have control over your business and you're working your tail off but not getting anywhere, this white paper will show you why that happens and what you can do to fix it. This is about working "on" your business, not just "in" it. If you want to grow your business, then you have to grow in your position as business owner. This is how you do it!

Strategy 2: The Opportunities List. 45

Do you know why people spend so much time spinning their wheels? It's because they don't have structure in their strategic planning. They just go out and start new projects before they even realized the benefits of the projects they've been working on. That results in a whole lot of "getting started" and not a lot of "getting it done." The Opportunities List is a great tool that will help you move in a straight line toward your objectives. If you crave structure in your business development instead of constant chaos, you'll love this white paper and action steps.

Strategy 3: Building Your Executive Team 55

Many business owners try to do everything themselves. That's too bad because that means the business can never be bigger than the owner. It creates an environment where profits suffer, company value is diminished, and good people eventually need to escape so they can meet their own potential. It also creates a scenario where the owner never has the freedom to come and go as he or she pleases. This white paper will help you create an executive team and then give you effective strategies on how to lead your leaders. When you implement the action steps from this white paper, you'll be well on your way to building a culture of accountability where the business is valuable and profitable whether you're there or not. By the way, *not* doing this stuff will result in a very low sale price for your business if you ever want to sell it. What a wasted opportunity. Don't let that happen!

Strategy 4: Every Brain in the Game 77

Do your employees remind you of the "walking dead"? What do your employees think about you? Do you know what's important to your people? Do they know what's important to you, and do they care? If you want to build an environment where people work in synchronicity, fueled with passion and enthusiasm, then you need to get every brain in the game. This white paper will show you how to get your team engaged and keep them engaged. This is a great first step in building a fantastic company culture based on trust, accountability, and excellence. But here's a warning for you: It all starts with you and it's not going to be quick or easy. It's going to require time, effort, and care. You'll get out of this equal to what you put in. If you just go through the motions, you'll probably do more damage than good. But if you commit to this and fully engage in it yourself, it will work beautifully. By the way, this is where the rubber meets the road, so you better have a strong executive team working with you so this can be a huge success for you, your team, and your company as a whole.

Strategy 5: People Problems 99

I think this is the single biggest area where business owners mess themselves and their companies up. In my opinion, people problems are the single biggest profit killer there is. And yet, we ignore them! Business owners bury their heads in the proverbial sand when it comes to dealing with people problems. This white paper identifies the different people problems that are common in companies (you'll recognize them, believe me!). It goes on to tell why business owners don't address these problems and why that is so costly. But don't worry, then we'll show you how you can immediately begin the process of fixing the people problems in your company. When you implement the action steps at the end of this white paper, you'll be on your way to building a stronger team and you'll be much more respected by your best people for having the courage to stand up for what is right in a classy, respectful way.

Strategy 6: Put Your Payroll on a Diet!. 109

Sometimes, our good intentions end up hurting us. Compounding that, sometimes we inadvertently set up the very people we're trying to be good to! There's nothing more critical to a company's success than its people, but we have to be careful that we don't allow our labor costs to get out of whack with what's appropriate. This white paper tells you why payroll gets fat and what to do to fix it and prevent it from happening again. If payroll is among your top single expense lines on your income statement, this is worth your time and attention!

Strategy 7: Finding and Filling the Profit Holes . . . 121

Large, gaping profit holes are generally easy to identify. Since they cost so much and are so glaringly visible, we fix them right away. But smaller, less visible, and less expensive profit holes often go unaddressed. Taken alone, none of these little profit holes has a terrible impact on our businesses, but collectively, they amount to a small fortune! This white paper shows you how to use your company's income statement as a tool in helping you identify the many little areas your company burns money on a regular basis. If your profit margin is not where you want it to be, this may be a great place for you to start to turn that around. The benefits of this white paper and the associated action steps can provide you a huge increase in profits and profit margin for years to come. This is great stuff!

Strategy 8: Improving Outside Sales 139

If you have outside salespeople in your company, then you've probably been on the receiving end of this comment: "It's on the fence. It'll probably land this week. Just give me a little more time." But it never lands. In fact, nothing seems to land! It seems like you're listening to a broken record of false optimism. But you don't know what to do.

Maybe the salesperson is right; maybe it is about to land. And you need sales badly. You've already invested a lot of time and money into your salesperson, so what can you do? You have to continue to wait, don't you? Nope. You don't. And if your salespeople aren't getting the results you need, then you can rest assured that this problem won't fix itself. There are specific reasons salespeople seem to work so hard but don't get the results you expect. And the good news is there's a lot you can do about it. Whether you've been a salesperson yourself or not, this white paper will give you some ideas to help you get your salespeople earning better results. Read this white paper, do the action steps, and get things right. Salespeople cannot be an expense to your company; they have to provide a return on investment. These strategies and action steps will help you be able to help your salespeople get the results you're looking for.

Strategy 9: Rallying Your Team around a Goal. . . 157

Yeah, I know. Goals are silly and they don't work. But the thing is: they do work! The reason most people don't benefit from goals is because they don't really have goals. They have snazzy hopes, but not true goals. This white paper is not a feel-good paper on goals. It's the real deal on how to set a goal, how to get your team behind it, and what you need to do to make sure everyone stays after it until the goal is met. I'll tell you right now, it's not easy, and it will require you to have a burning desire to achieve your goal or it won't work. But if you're ready to start hitting your goals on a regular basis and it is worth the effort to you, then this will prepare you with everything you need to make that happen. The weak-willed need not apply! This is for people who are driven to succeed.

Strategy 10: Vision, Mission, Values Statements . . . 173

I'm not talking about the spider-webbed covered plaques that hang lonely in a company lobby! You know the ones, full of platitudes and fluff that don't even resemble how the company really operates. Instead, I'm talking about vision, mission, and values statements that guide behavior. They're the basis for strategic decisions. They determine who gets hired, who gets promoted, and who gets canned. We've all used the expression, "We have to get on the same page." Well, this is the page! If you're not using this tool or using it correctly, you're missing a fantastic opportunity and it's costing you money, energy, and emotion and your best people aren't being served. Really, it's time for you and your team to get on the same page together. This is how you do it. The results are just too big to ignore.

Strategy 11: The Great Huddle 189

AKA your staff meeting. But not just the normal, run-of-the-mill, useless, waste-of-time staff meetings. But first, please allow a note: I "borrowed" the name "The Great Huddle" from Jack Stack from his book (and one of my all-time favorites), *The Great Game of Business*. Hopefully, by sincerely plugging his book, Mr. Stack will give me a pass on swiping his cool lingo. The Great Huddle is a staff meeting that people will actually look forward to. They're enjoyable and productive. They're meaningful, and they provide a return on your investment of time, money, and effort. This white paper shows you how to create extremely effective staff meetings and gives you specific action steps so you can benefit from The Great Huddle at your company. The result is improved communication and teamwork among your people. That improves effectiveness and accountability for results. It also breeds a culture of excellence that will make your company stand out among your competitors who still demoralize and annoy their teams with lousy staff meetings.

Strategy 12: Systems Through Standard Operating Procedures 207

Imagine how chaotic it would be to drive to work if there weren't traffic systems in place that we all understood and abided by. Of course, there would be more accidents. There would also be variation in how long it took you to get to work. Some days, your drive would be efficient; other days would take longer. One thing's for sure: there would be a lot more stress and confusion. Well, the same is true in your business. If you don't have systems that guide your people and your operations, then you have stress, confusion, accidents, waste, and inefficiency that eat your profits and tick off your customers. If you want to increase your profits, decrease waste, improve quality, and make your company much more valuable, then you need to make sure your company is systematized. This white paper shows you how do it and then suggests action steps to get you moving toward realizing the significant benefits provided through systems.

Strategy 13: Personal Effectiveness. 217

When is the last time you took time to evaluate specifically where you are in your life right now compared to where you'd like to be? With all of the demands on your time and energy, it's difficult to live life "intentionally." Instead, we just "crank it out" day after day. This strategy will show you how to identify the gaps of where you are now versus where you want to be in your personal life. Then, you will prioritize which area to focus on first that will have the greatest impact on your overall health and happiness. You will determine strategies and tactics to begin to live more intentionally. By the time you're done with this chapter, you'll have specific action steps for yourself that you can take within the next seven days to begin the journey toward closing that most important gap in your personal life. There are no quick fixes, but there is a gentle, controlled approach to continuous personal development that can have a tremendously favorable impact on your overall health and happiness. This works.

Bonus: The "Not-So-Smart" Things
I've Done or Seen 227

This bonus chapter includes some not-so-smart things I've done as a business owner and some not-so-smart things I haven't done, but have seen other business owners do (Yes, that's my story and I'm sticking to it!). Hopefully, you'll either learn or be reminded of some not-so-smart stuff that you'll benefit from *not* doing!

Thirteen business strategies along with *specific action steps* to help serious business owners earn more money, have more time, and significantly increase company value.

Because without action, nothing happens!

STRATEGY 1

MY COMPANY OWNS ME

How many business owners out there feel like your entire company rests squarely on your shoulders and you're back is breaking under the pressure?

If you feel this way, then I know who you are. You're the person whose dream of owning and running a business has turned into a nightmare.

You're overworked. You can't come and go as you please. All of your company's different problems ultimately land on you to fix. You're burned out and your personal life is affected. You're frustrated. You're tired. You're surrounded by people, but you feel very alone. You are stuck.

First off, let me tell you that you're not alone. In fact, you're in the majority of small business owners that have become owned by their businesses. Here's some great news: you can fix it!

You're probably thinking, "Yeah, right. Give me another thing to do. I have no money, no time, and no belief that this can change. I'm stuck and there's nothing I can do about it." Please keep reading.

Think back to the day your company was created in your mind. For those of you that grew up in a family business, think back to the day before you took the reins. No matter how long ago that may have been, the significance of how you were feeling and what you were thinking were emotional enough that you can remember.

Were you thinking about creating a business where your employees would love their jobs? Were you excited about providing such outstanding products or services that your customers would trumpet your name to all their friends and business would boom? Did you think about how different you would be from past bosses you had that sucked all the air out of the room when they walked in? Sure you did!

You were also thinking about how much money you would make and how generous you would be with your team. You would put in a few great years, then work shorter days so you could coach your son's little league team or your daughter's soccer team. Ah, yes, the long weekends at your camp and two vacations every year in the Caribbean! At the end of it all, you thought, you'd have a company worth millions of dollars. Life was great and you were ready!

And for the first few years, you gladly worked your tail off. You didn't mind working nights or weekends if needed. After all, it was a good way to keep payroll down. You made the sales calls, served your customers, and even worked in production. You did the purchasing and paid the bills. You made the collection calls and did the hiring. You were chief cook and bottle washer and didn't mind because you knew, you absolutely *knew* it would all pay off in the end.

But as the years continued to pass, you started to burn out. You tried to hire some great people to help you, but people always let you down. You didn't blame them; deep inside you knew you hadn't interviewed enough people to find the right fit. You never even called the references that were provided. And after you made a hire, you didn't have time or even a system to train your new employees. They were thrown to the wolves! But it didn't work and nothing was done correctly. If you wanted something done right, you just had to do it yourself. So you did…and you still do.

Sound familiar? If so, here's the problem in a nutshell: *Your business is still operating as a start-up company even though it's several years old.* Think about it:

- How much leadership depth have you built?

- What systems do you have in place to maximize efficiencies?

- How much of your time do you spend handling tasks that someone else could handle for you at a fraction of your pay?

- How much (or how little) of your own time is spent developing your team?

- Are you working "on" your business, or are you still working "in" the business?

- Does everybody have written job descriptions and a clear understanding of their roles and responsibilities?

- Who holds them accountable for results?

- Do you have a formal training program in place for new hires?

- What about developmental training for your existing employees?

- What have you done in past years for your own professional development?

- Is everyone on the same page?

- Do your individual team members (employees) know why the company exists?

- Do they know why you started it in the first place?

- Do they know what it's *supposed* to look like?

- Do you know your employees' goals?

- Do they know yours?

- Do they know what's in it for them (beyond just a paycheck)?

- Do they understand how a business makes money?

- Are they in tune enough with your business to be able to identify and fix the many little operational holes that money pours through every single month?

- Do your customers still feel as loved by you as they used to?

- Have you taken them for granted in recent years?

- When's the last time you talked to your best customers about *their* businesses?

- Do you know what their challenges are?

- Do you know what their goals are?

- What do they love about your product or service?

- How would they improve it if they could?

Here's an important question to ask to see if you're still operating as a start-up business: "What would happen to your company if you stopped working there today?"

Okay, those are twenty-seven pretty darn good questions that all need to be answered. But you don't have time to find the answers to these questions, and worse yet, if you had the answers to those questions, you'd know you have a lot more work to do! You certainly don't have time for more work!

Here is the most important question: If you don't answer those questions, and address those issues, who will?

You already know the answer: nobody.

And that's precisely why you feel the way you do today. Instead of leading your business, developing it, and nurturing it, you work *in* it. You're just as task oriented as you were in the early days of your business.

Do you know why an athletic coach doesn't score points or block shots during a game? Because it's not his job! His job is to recruit talent and make sure his team is agile and skilled, has depth, takes initiative, works in synchronicity, and is prepared to win games. His job is the same is yours. Think about that!

You have to figure out how to get out of the proverbial trees and work on the forest.

Here's your first action step: Read the book *The E-Myth Revisited* by Michael Gerber. It's an easy read and is even enjoyable! Most importantly, though, it will clearly show you the problems many business owners make and how to start to solve them.

Moving your business from infancy to adolescence to maturity (your vision) will take time and effort. Like all meaningful transitions, it takes patience and care. It won't happen all at once; it will require many small steps.

Listen, you deserve the fruits of your risk and your labor. Take the first step: read the book. Then, decide on your next step. Maybe that will be to make a list of the things you can easily pass off to someone else to do. The next step: pass those things off accordingly!

When that's done, the next step will appear to you, but could include:

- Writing a vision/mission/values document

- Writing comprehensive job descriptions and developing a formal organizational chart so everyone's clear on their roles and responsibilities

- Scheduling and conducting regular performance evaluations

- Creating or outsourcing the creation of a training program for new hires

- Scheduling appointments to reconnect with your customers

- Creating an operations manual for your business (systems/procedures)
- Brainstorming your company goals with your team and creating a bonus game around meeting those goals
- Revamping your interviewing process and hiring procedures
- Outsourcing the redesign of your marketing material
- Enrolling in a leadership development program
- The list of possibilities is endless!

If you involve your team in the process, you'll get some great input and differing points of view to consider. Furthermore, your team can take steps for you and they'll appreciate the opportunity to show you how valuable they are.

Don't let tomorrow be a continuation of the same old story! Stop the madness today by taking action! It won't be easy, but you can do it!

REVIEW / ACTION STEPS

1. Read the book *The E-Myth Revisited* by Michael Gerber. The reason you should read this book is because you will learn different strategies for taking your business from infancy to adolescence to maturity. You'll also learn why it's valuable to create a cookie-cutter approach (called the franchise model, without having to

be a franchise) in order to eliminate variation in your products or service and so you can run your business most efficiently, which results in higher profits. This book is a classic.

2. Make a list of the things you're currently doing yourself that you could pass off to someone else to do—including outsourcing business functions—so you can free up some of your time to work on your business. Then, pass those things off! As you're doing this, you may be tempted to not pass something off because nobody can do certain things as well as you do. Don't let that stop you! There's a reason nobody can do certain things as well as you can; they don't have the experience you do. And they'll never get that experience until you give them the opportunity. So do it! Mistakes will happen, but that's okay. In the end, you'll have a business that can run without you, and that is how you create a business that works for you and is also much more valuable than one that requires you. Remember, if your business requires you, then you don't own the business any more than it owns you!

   Once you free up some time for yourself to be able to work on important business owner duties, continue to 3 below.

3. Answer the following questions, then prioritize them in order of importance, and then create action steps for yourself so that you can begin working on your top priority areas. The goal is

for you to answer all of these questions and get the answer you most desire. You need to create a plan to make that happen. It won't happen overnight, not even close! You also can't do it all at once, so it's important that you focus on just one or two of these areas at any one time. This is a never-ending process that you should pay attention to and reevaluate regularly. Here are the questions:

- How much leadership depth have you built? If your answer is, "Not much," then what are you going to do about it? What action step can you give yourself that will immediately start building leadership depth in your business?

- What systems do you have in place to maximize efficiencies? You probably have systems in place, but when is the last time you analyzed all of those systems to see if you can improve on them? Also, when mistakes happen in your business, do you always ask yourself, "Was this mistake made because we don't have a system in place, or was this mistake made because our system wasn't followed, or did this mistake happen because our system failed and needs to be reworked?" What action step can you give yourself to make your systems work even better for you than they currently are?

- How much of your time do you spend handling tasks that someone else could handle for you at a fraction of your pay? It's highly unlikely that you're paying yourself as an hourly employee, but it is important that you calculate your effective hourly rate so you know how much your own personal time costs you each hour. Also, as you're answering this question, you may want to calculate your hourly pay based on how much money you want to be earning within the next year rather than how much you're currently earning. You also may want to calculate your hourly pay based on a forty-hour work week even if you're currently working much more than that. After all, if you were an hourly employee, you'd be getting paid for every hour you work plus time and a half for every hour over forty hours you work in a week! Don't fool yourself into thinking your extra time is free because it's not. You're paying for it one way or another! Once you do this, please make a list of all the things you're currently doing that you can find someone else to do at a fraction of your pay. You're doing this so that you'll have more time available to work on important strategic business development initiatives rather than simply working as an employee in your own business. Once you have the master list of all the things you're currently doing that you should pass off to someone else, ask yourself what action step(s) you can give yourself to begin the process of freeing up your time.

- Does everybody have written job descriptions and a clear understanding of their roles and responsibilities? If not, they need to! Written job descriptions not only bring clarity to what's expected of people, but they can also be used to develop formal training programs. They're also important tools to reference when conducting employee reviews. By attaching responsibilities to the job descriptions, people will better understand how they fit into the big picture. For example, after every duty listed in a person's job description (i.e., Be able to produce 100 widgets per hour with a 99.7 percent accuracy rating), be sure to explain how this fits in the big picture (i.e., So that our production department can run profitably while client deadlines are met 100 percent of the time.) Do you currently have job descriptions? Are they complete? How can you improve them? Once you have those questions answered, ask yourself one more question: What is the first action step I should take to begin the process of developing valuable job descriptions for every position we employ?

- Who holds people accountable for results? Let's face it: people do what you measure. If there's no accountability, then responsibilities become optional, at least in the minds of extrinsically motivated people. But when there's follow-up and accountability, people are more driven to produce. I'm pretty sure we all know that, but does your company have a culture of accountability? Can you improve on it? If so, what's the smartest action step you can take in your business to improve personal accountability for delivering quality results?

- Do you have a formal training program in place for new hires? At a minimum, this should include an explanation of your company history, your vision, mission, and values statements, your company goals, a workflow overview of your entire operations, a thorough review of the written job description, HR policies and procedures, an introduction to department leaders throughout your company, and a comprehensive checklist of necessary training components so that your new hires can be trained systematically and thoroughly. If you do not have a formal training program in place, what action steps can you give yourself to begin the process of creating one? If you already have a formal training program but think it needs to be updated, what is the next most important action step you can give yourself to begin the process of improving your current training program for new hires?

- What about developmental training for your existing employees? One of the biggest investments in your business is labor costs. It's very likely that payroll is the single largest expense in your business. Shouldn't you do all you can to make sure you're getting the biggest return on that investment? Of course! So please make sure you're providing developmental training for your people. They'll get better at their jobs and be able to contribute more to your company. They win, you win. Your people will make or break your business. Field the best team you can and then invest in helping them grow technologically, in leadership, in strategic thinking and planning, and in product knowledge. If you believe that your company can benefit by providing valuable developmental training for your people, what specifically should you do? What action step(s) can you give yourself to either begin the process or improve your processes in fielding a smarter, more talented team of people?

- What have you done in past years for your own professional development? Since you're reading this right now, then clearly you are working on your professional development. If this is a new commitment you're making for yourself and your company, then congratulations! There absolutely will be a return on your investment of time, money, and effort. If this is a renewed commitment to your own professional development, then welcome back! Stick with it. You're leading by example and by expanding your own capacity, you're simultaneously expanding the capacity of your business. If this is a continuation of a commitment to your constant professional development, that's great. You get it. Please remember, the results of your efforts are cumulative. You'll never completely master "business ownership" and "business development" because there's always more to do, but you'll continually improve and your company will follow suit. From time to time, be sure to ask yourself, "I wonder what my competitors are doing right now?" Chances are they're just trying to get through the day today, and tomorrow will just be a continuation of the same old story! But your continued learning will translate into fueled energy, which will result in actions that will create the results you desire. Can you think of any specific areas you could benefit from professional development other than what you're currently doing? If so, what action step can you give yourself to begin the process of making that happen?

- Is everyone on the same page? That's not a figurative page, it's a literal page. The page is your vision, mission, values statements that your team is accountable to. Please consider the importance of your team having an actual document that aligns everyone in terms of goals, purpose, strategies, tactics, and culture. How could that impact your culture, your customer service, your quality, and your brand? If you do not currently have a vision, mission, values statement that guides your company and is used as a management tool, then as an action step, please read Strategy 10 in this book! At the end of that white paper, you will be provided a series of action steps that will guide you in developing a meaningful vision, mission, values statement for your company.

- Do your individual team members (employees) know why the company exists? "Why" is very important! People are more focused and will be more committed when they know why. What is your vision, and what are your core values? Why are those important? Why did you make the decision to start this company in the first place? What is special about your company, and why is that important? What do your customers value? What should your team members expect beyond just a paycheck when your vision is achieved? What does a company win look like and why is that important? It is a leader's job to help the team get clarity of purpose. If you think your team is fuzzy about all the whys in your company, then please make a list of all the things you want them to understand. Make a list of all the whys you want to share with them, and then, take the next step (whatever you determine that should be) to execute your plan of helping your team understand the whys. When your team understands why, they'll appreciate the dignity you've shown them and will be more focused on the big picture as they work through the days.

• Do you know your employees' goals? Why is that important? Because people don't care how much you know until they know how much you care about them. When you know what your people are trying to accomplish in their own lives, then you can help them discover how to meet those goals by performing well within your organization. And as they move closer to their own goals, you'll undoubtedly move closer to yours as a result of your individual team member's contributions and personal/professional growth. Everyone has to win! Furthermore, when you invest time into learning about the people you employ, you will strengthen your relationships with those people. I know there are a lot of business leaders that shy away from (or even laugh at) soft leadership skills (as they're called). But here's a fact: your people are far less likely to care about your goals if you don't care enough to know theirs. If you haven't talked with every single person you employ to find out what's important to them in their own lives, then please give yourself an action step to begin the process of doing that. It's time-consuming, but by the time you're done, you will have strengthened every relationship you have with your individual team members. I guarantee each will go home after work and tell someone about the experience that was so meaningful to them! You will make a difference.

• Does your team know your personal goals? When you share your own goals with your team, you'll build trust by connecting with your people. When you care about someone, you'll do whatever you can to help them achieve their goals and you'll celebrate with them when they win. If you have the right people on your team, they'll be fueled with passion to help you achieve your goals, especially if you return the favor and do the same for them! I would suggest that before you make it a point to tell everyone your own personal goals, you should learn theirs first. What should you do to begin or expand on the benefits of sharing personal goals within your team?

• Do they know what's in it for them (beyond just a paycheck)? What do you think would happen if your people were just in it for the money and your toughest competitor offered them each an additional 50 cents an hour to come over to their place? I guarantee you'd lose most, if not all of them. Employment can't just be about a paycheck or your people will look at their work as a commodity. Instead, allow your people to be part of the entire process so they can meet their own needs relative to personal and professional growth opportunities, recognition, and purpose. Jack Welch (former chairman of GE) said, "You pay a person for his or her hands, but they'll give you their hearts and minds for free…all you have to do is ask!" Why would people give their hearts and minds for free? Because they want to! It's meaningful to them. And what's the result for you? A passionate team working with energy of purpose to make your company even more successful. So why wouldn't you go out of your way to give your people the opportunity to be part of something much bigger than themselves individually? Using the Visa Card tagline: "Your paycheck is $X. But personal and professional growth, recognition, and purpose: Priceless!" If you haven't articulated what's in it for your team beyond the paychecks, what can you do to start the process of letting them know that? If you aren't sure what things "beyond a paycheck" are important to your team members, then I suggest you simply ask them! There's your action step!

- Do the people you employ understand how a business makes money? It's obvious to business owners how a business makes money or loses it. You see the income statement and you sign the checks. You know how much it costs to produce your product or service. You know the difference between gross profit margin and net profit margin. You know the impacts of insurance costs, taxes, repairs, maintenance, marketing, legal costs, accounting costs, production waste, and other costs that are often invisible to your team members. And you may think your team members know all this too. But the fact is they probably don't. They don't know because you haven't shown them! When you teach your team about how a company makes money, you'll arm them with an awareness that will make them sensitive to the importance of every dollar and every decision. Otherwise, people may think that a dollar here and there doesn't really make a difference to a big company like yours! As an action step, I strongly suggest you read the book, *The Great Game of Business*, by Jack Stack. Once you do that, go ahead and put your new or refreshed knowledge into action! The result of this will be a cadre of employees who will be much more in tune in identifying and fixing the many little operational holes that money pours through each month. This can be incredibly valuable information for you to have and your people will feel good about themselves when they make contributions to improve your company. Again, everyone wins!

• Do your customers still feel as loved by you as they used to? Have you taken them for granted in recent years? Those two questions go hand-in-hand. It's natural for people to take what was once a blessing and grow so accustomed to it that they end up taking it for granted. You know the old saying: "You don't know what you've got until it's gone." And that can cost you dearly in business and in life. So make sure those long-time friends (customers) still feel how special they are to you. What action step(s) can you give yourself so that you can be sure your customers are still feeling valued by you and your company?

• When's the last time you talked to your best customers about their business? Do you know what their challenges are? Do you know what their goals are? What do they love about your product or service? How would they improve it if they could? Imagine how powerful it would be if you understood your customers' business challenges. You would relate to them on a whole new level. With that information, you may be able to customize your product or service to help them solve their problems. Or maybe your billing practices, ordering procedures, quality control, or delivery practices could be improved upon to add more value to your customers. A lot of business owners struggle to think of how they can improve their value proposition and better differentiate their businesses from the competition. But why guess when all you have to do is ask? When you understand your customers' businesses, their goals, and the challenges they have, you'll become much less a commodity and much more a value driver. For decades, we've heard businesses say they partner with their customers. Really? Honestly, ask yourself the question that is in bold print at the top of this paragraph and then ask yourself: "Are we really partners, or am I just a vendor?" What action step(s) can you give yourself to begin the process of learning more about your customers' thoughts, feelings, ideas, opinions, issues, goals, etc.?

• What would happen to your company if you stopped working there today? If the answer to that question is, "My company would fold," then you haven't really built a business. Instead, you've built a job for yourself. This means that the value of your company to someone else is diminished to the amount they'd be willing to pay for your fixed assets and for having the ability to have your job. I know that's a bit of an overstatement, but truly, if you don't have depth and if your business is 100 percent dependent on you, then you don't own your business any more than it owns you. There's no freedom in that, and honestly, you're diminishing your company's value significantly. If this describes your company, then here's your action step: Make a list of all the reasons why your company would fold if you went away. Then, work with your team and/or a business coach or trusted advisor to help you create and then execute a plan to make the business less dependent on you. If you've raised kids, then you already have experience doing this, unless your thirty-four-year-old is still living in your basement with no intentions of ever moving out!

- What other business development opportunities do you have in front of you? You know your business better than anyone. Ask yourself, "What is the most important thing I can invest time in to help get my business to where I want it to be?" Once you've identified that critical initiative, give yourself the smartest next step you have to take to begin the process of meeting that opportunity!

SUMMARY

When you own a business, there's always work to do. Work surrounds you! The art of being a great small business owner is in deciding what is important for you to do and what is better left for someone else to do.

As CEO, your job is to build and develop your company, not to make the products or deliver the services your company sells. When your business is brand-new, you'll be intimately involved in producing and delivering what your company sells. But in order for your business to move from start-up mode to adolescence and then to maturity, you have to change your focus.

For example, if you own an electrical contracting business, your focus needs to be on building that business, not in being an electrician. Otherwise, all you've done is create a job for yourself. In his book, *The E-Myth Revisited*, Michael Gerber continues that thought by saying, "And you work for a lunatic!"

It's natural for business owners to work in the business instead of on it because that's what's familiar to them. The electrical contractor business-owner is a great electrician, but has no training or experience in being a business owner. Therefore, he does what he knows instead of learning and then executing what he must do to build a profitable, valuable company.

You already know what the result of that mismanagement leads to: working too hard and sacrificing too much for too little in return. That's not why you went into business!

This white paper identified some great first steps to move you from being what Michael Gerber calls a technician to what he refers to as the entrepreneur.

By identifying a couple things you currently do and deciding to pass those things off to someone else to handle, you have freed up precious time for yourself. Then you identified the top two or three business development initiatives that will be most beneficial to your company. Finally, you created action steps to begin working on those important business development initiatives. Those are the things that would never happen without your personal direction and oversight.

As you find success in these initiatives, continue to repeat this process. Revisit this white paper from time to time. It suggests several important CEO initiatives that are commonly overlooked by business owners.

By staying focused and continuing to take the proper actions, your company can become mature, profitable, valuable, and an absolute joy for you to own.

Go take action and get unstuck!

STRATEGY 2

THE OPPORTUNITIES LIST

Imagine if you always had a written list of all the things that are standing between where you are now and where you want to be (your goals). This is a running list of all of the opportunities or problems to be solved in your company.

And imagine if this list was constantly prioritized (and re-prioritized) so you'd always be working on the most important things. You would refer to the list frequently to create specific action steps for yourself (and your team) to solve problems and reach your goals. Sounds pretty useful, doesn't it?

Well, such a list does (or can) exist! We call it "The Opportunities List." In his book, *Traction*, author Gino Wickman calls this an "Issues List." (By the way, I strongly recommend that you read Wickman's book and apply his principles. They're outstanding!)

When you have an active list of all the problems, issues, challenges, and opportunities in your company, you have a comprehensive blueprint of specifically what you should be focusing your efforts on in order to maximize the profitability and value of your company.

The first step in benefitting from an Opportunities List is to create the initial list. This is not a task-oriented to-do list. It's a listing of the major initiatives that your company needs to undertake in order to solve your problems or capitalize on your opportunities.

Think of every problem you have in your company and write them down. These problems could include lack of profits, mistakes your company makes, people problems, lack of cash, accounts receivable issues, facility maintenance problems, lack of sales, customer issues, and any and all other problems you have in your company.

Then think of every opportunity your company could benefit from and put those on your list. Your opportunities could include creating a better onboarding program for new hires, enhancing your sales and marketing efforts, expanding your business either geographically or in product/service offerings, creating a company-wide operations manual, providing leadership development training for your key people, and any and all other opportunities that can make your company stronger.

By the end of this initial exercise, it's likely you'll have a long list of problems, issues, and opportunities within your company. That's valuable because before you can fix a problem, you first have to clearly identify what needs to be fixed!

Now it's time to prioritize your list. After all, it's not practical to think you can solve all of your problems and capitalize on all of your opportunities at once. Nobody has the time to do that. So instead, prioritize your list according to importance.

What items should be your top priorities? That completely depends on the state of your business. For example, let's presume that "slow-paying customers" is on your list, but your current and projected cash position is healthy. At the same time, "production errors are costing us customers" is also on your list. Since this problem is costing you valuable customers, your priority should probably be focused first around improving your quality before addressing your problem with slow-paying customers. It's not a matter of generic importance; it's a matter of *situational* importance.

Just to be clearer with an obvious example: If you were fifty pounds overweight and you just cut your finger wide open, the priority would be to "stop the bleeding" before you plan and then execute your new exercise regimen and healthier eating plans! Yes, both are important, but timing is everything! Always stop the bleeding first! (I mean that literally *and* figuratively!)

Once you have thoughtfully prioritized your top three to five problems or opportunities, it's time to create specific *action steps* around solving the problems or capitalizing on those opportunities.

For example, let's suppose you created your master Opportunities List and then you prioritized it. Let's suppose the top three opportunities you identified as being the highest priority are:

1. We don't have goals.

2. We need better office administration.

3. Cash flow is tight.

Now it's time to go through these opportunities one by one and determine the smartest next steps that need to be taken in order to capitalize on each of these high-priority opportunities and/or problems.

To continue this example, let's start with the number one opportunity listed above: We don't have goals.

As you and your senior leaders strategize around that opportunity, you may determine that the best next step you can take is to schedule a time to work together on setting thoughtful goals. So your action step my look like this: "Our executive team is going to meet on Tuesday, May 31 from 6:00 p.m. to 8:30 p.m. to work on setting our five-year goal (long-term), three-year goal (mid-term), and our goal for this year (annual goal). When we've completed that, we'll break our annual goal down into monthly guidepost goals, so we can make sure we're moving at the right pace toward our annual goal."

Perfect! First, you identified all of your problems and opportunities. Then you determined your top-priority opportunity: "We need goals." Then you brainstormed a solution: "We need to set goals." And finally, you took the next step in getting that done: "Our meeting is scheduled and the objectives of that meeting are stated: 'We're going to set our goals.'"

Obviously, the next thing you would do to capitalize on this opportunity is to actually have the meeting, do the work, and come away with a long-term goal, mid-term goal, an annual goal, and monthly goals.

Once that's done, further actions may appear to you. For example, the next action step might be, "At our

June 13 staff meeting, we'll let everyone know what we came up with for goals and we'll get their feedback. If need be, we'll modify the goals. The objectives of the June 13 staff meeting is to leave that meeting with (1) agreement on what our goals are and (2) for everyone on our team to know what the goals are. If we have time, we'll strategize with our team specifically what we need to do to reach these goals and will add those ideas to our Opportunities List."

And then you continue the process of moving this opportunity forward until you can receive tangible benefits from your initiatives!

But remember, while all this goal-setting and goal-reaching work is going on, you and your executive team will also begin work on the other top priorities on your Opportunities List.

Using our example above, you may decide the next step in fixing the number two priority-opportunity ("We need better office administration.") is, "Jennifer will meet with Paul tomorrow to have a candid discussion with him about his performance and to determine a specific and measurable plan for improvement." Of course, after that action step is completed, another action step may become necessary to continue solving the original problem.

For priority three ("Cash flow is tight."), you may decide that the next best step is, "Jim will call the bank tomorrow to start the process of getting an increase in our line of credit. Within the next two days, Jill will send statements to all of our customers with receivables over forty days old and will start making collection calls to these people next week." Once that's done, you'll determine the next action step necessary in solving your cash flow problem.

As you can see, the Opportunities List is a great tool in keeping you focused on specifically what you should do next.

Throughout the days, weeks, and months, new opportunities will undoubtedly push their way up to the top of your priority list. In other words, stuff will happen that you'll need to address immediately. Just put it on the top of your Opportunities List and get on about fixing it! You don't need to worry that other initiatives you've identified or even started on will be forgotten; they're written down. As long as you continuously review your Opportunities List, prioritize and reprioritize, and continually create specific action steps (with deadlines) to capitalize on your opportunities, your company will be in perpetual business development mode and your results will always be improving.

The Opportunities List is not a hard tool to use. It does require time, effort, creativity, and discipline. But the benefits are incredible and well worth the investment of time and effort.

Take action and go get yourself unstuck!

REVIEW / ACTION STEPS

1. Work with your leadership team, a business coach, or a trusted advisor to create your Opportunities List. This is the list of all of the things that are standing in the way of where

you are now to where you want to be (your vision). In other words, make a list of all your opportunities, problems, challenges, issues, or whatever you choose to call them!

2. Prioritize your list and determine the top two or three things you should work on first to have the most dramatically favorable impact on your business.

3. Beginning with your top priority problem or opportunity, determine the most important first steps you can take and create action steps with deadlines.

4. Complete your action steps! Remember, nothing happens without action.

5. Determine the next steps you have to make to continue moving forward toward solving the problem or capitalizing on the opportunity and then complete those action steps. Continue to repeat this process until your problem is solved and/or the opportunity is met.

6. Important tip: Even though you may refer to your Opportunities List on a daily basis, please schedule a recurring time *each week* to dedicate to (1)reviewing and re-prioritizing your opportunities, (2) measuring the results of past action steps, (3) adjusting your plans as necessary, and (4) creating new action steps (with deadlines) to keep things moving forward.

SUMMARY

An Opportunities List is a great tool to help you make strategic and tactical decisions so that you can capitalize on opportunities and solve the problems within your company.

If you don't use a tool like this, you'll be like most business owners that spend their days "putting out fires" instead of strategically planning to prevent those fires from occurring or reoccurring in the first place. There's no need for that!

If you want to continue to enhance your company's value and maximize your profits, then you have to do things differently than you've done them to this point. Creating and then using an Opportunities List provides a regimented, disciplined, proactive approach to business improvement and development.

It's also a great tool that will assist you in working on your business rather than simply working in your business. That results in your ability to have more control over your business rather than the other way around.

It's really a simple concept: (1) determine every problem and unmet opportunity you have in your company, (2) prioritize the problems or opportunities, (3) identify your top three to five prioritized problems / opportunities, (4) brainstorm solutions to fix them or capitalize on them, and then (5) create specific action steps that can immediately be implemented to start the process of getting things the way you want them to be.

As you do this, other problems or opportunities in your business will surface. Put them on the list and repeat the process of prioritizing, brainstorming, and creating action steps to address your issues.

Please remember that you have to see things all the way through to completion; otherwise, all of the work put into solving a problem or capitalizing on an opportunity may be lost. If you have to put an initiative on the back burner due to a new problem that's surfaced, do it. But don't forget to come back to that initial problem when you're able to so you can complete the process and reap the benefits of all your efforts.

As simple as it is, using an Opportunities List requires time, attention, and care. But it's a fantastic way to maintain control of your business and to maximize value and profits. Please be sure your executive team is involved in identifying the issues, prioritizing the initiatives, and creating the action plans which they will help you with. Business development is a team sport!

Go get unstuck!

STRATEGY 3

BUILDING YOUR
EXECUTIVE TEAM

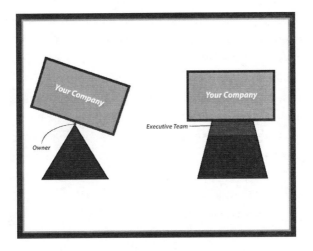

Please look at the illustrations above. Most privately owned businesses look like the picture on the left. Why is the company tilted? Because the business is too big for one person to try to balance! If almost everything in your company ultimately falls on you to handle, then that's what your company looks like. I feel badly for you! Look at all that weight on your shoulders! That's a lot of pressure. You probably don't get much time off, either. After all, if you were gone, what would happen to the company? Yup, it would fall down.

Go back to the picture on the right: That's what a stable company looks like. This business is strong and able to accommodate growth without anyone getting crushed. The company on the right is far more valuable, rewarding, and enjoyable to its owner than the one on the left.

The difference between the two pictures is simple: one has all the weight on the owner, the other has weight distributed among an executive team.

What is an executive team? It is a group of individual leaders in your company who are responsible for a division, or a department. In very small businesses, the entire department may be made up of just one person. In larger organizations, the departments have department heads with people that report directly to that person.

If you have an organizational chart, you can easily determine who those people are. They are the people named on the chart who oversee a division or department. If you don't have an organizational chart, then that's your first action step: you need to create one. If you're not sure how to do that, conduct an Internet search and you'll find a variety of different resources to help you.

Once you have your organizational chart in front of you, it will be easy for you determine who your executive team is, what they are in charge of, and who reports to each of your leaders.

Okay, to review, *who* is on your executive team? Your executive team is the group of people who are responsible for a particular division or department within your company. This could be your sales manager, production manager, manager of client services, controller, store or facility managers, marketing director, crew chiefs, vice presidents, etc.

Now that we have the "who" figured out, let's talk about *what* an executive team does. An executive team's job is to assist the owner (or CEO) in working on the business, as opposed to working in the business. The executive team helps the CEO create the company's goals and then transforms those goals into smart strategies. Then they break those overall strategies down into specific action steps. But that's not all; the executive team is also responsible for making sure the action steps that have been decided on are actually executed all the way to completion.

From a reporting standpoint: Each individual executive team member is accountable to the executive team as a whole and to the owner. The rank-and-file employees are accountable to their executive team representatives (department heads). This is referred to as the chain of command or the organizational hierarchy.

We've got the who and we've got the what. Now, let's address the "when" of the executive team. Your executive team should meet together privately and uninterrupted at a *minimum* of a couple hours per month. For bigger businesses, you'll likely spend even more time than that. But even the smallest businesses should allocate at least a couple hours every month to strategic planning, improving operating plans, reviewing past initiatives, and agreeing on the assignment of specific actions steps that will be accomplished before the next scheduled executive team meeting. If you're the only person in your company, you should still do this. Hire a professional business coach, meet with another business-owner friend, talk to your spouse about it, do whatever you need to do to make sure you spend this time working strategically on your business each month, but don't do it alone.

The best time to schedule executive team meetings are after-hours. During working hours, the phone is ringing, calls need to be returned, employees need to be coached, proposals are due, deadlines are pressing, business is happening! Don't let this critically important meeting interfere with your business operations. Instead, schedule it for an off-time when everyone can focus on the content of the meeting instead of stressing out about what they're currently *not* doing. Most businesses like to have after-hour meetings directly after work. That means you'll be cutting into dinnertime and you'll have some hungry execs. Buy them dinner! Believe me, it's worth the investment. It may even be nice to buy them a beer or glass of wine while you eat and meet.

Now I'll show you how an executive team works. Please note: to best illustrate how an executive team works, I'm going to create your hypothetical executive team that is working on a hypothetical objective to be capitalized on. Please do not get hung up on the specifics of the objective. Instead, please just focus on the process the hypothetical executive team is following.

In other words, this isn't about the specific objective; it's about "how" to operate as an executive team!

Let's say your company has the goal of increasing net profits by 5 percent over last year (that's the hypothetical objective I referenced above!). It's 6:00 p.m. on a Tuesday night and you and your executive team are having dinner in a place where you have privacy. After the exec team cracks a few jokes and tells some war stories from earlier in the day, you call the meeting to order. You let the executive team know that the company's profit margin is not where it needs to be and together, you're going to plan how to increase that margin by 5 percent over last year. You'll let them know that once the plans are drawn, together, you'll break down those plans into specific action steps that your executive team members will either execute themselves or delegate to others.

To begin the process of increasing your profit margin, you decide to start by asking the group to tell you where they see money being wasted (for example). One by one, each executive identifies what he or she thinks may be areas of waste in the entire company, not just in their own divisions!

As your exec team is brainstorming areas where money is wasted, you or another appointed exec is taking notes, ensuring that all of the ideas are written down. You can use an easel and flipchart if you'd like. The important thing is to make sure you keep great notes because after the meeting, these notes will be typed and distributed to the executive team members.

Now here's a very important point: It is not the business owner's job to have all the right answers; it's your job to ask the right questions! If you're the sole source of all the answers (as too many business owners are), the company can never grow larger than your own personal knowledge and opinions and at the same time, you're creating a business that is completely dependent on you; see the diagram at the beginning of this white paper, the one on the left? That poor business owner is the sole source of answers!

Once you ask your executive team to tell you where they see waste, and once you give them permission to speak freely, a good executive team will begin spewing their ideas, the ones that have likely been pent up inside of them for months, even years! If they remain quiet, it is your job to focus the question a little more for them. For example, instead of asking where they think money is wasted, ask, "Where do we have wasted labor? Where are we spending too much money? Who are our unprofitable customers? How much are we spending on redoing projects due to errors in production? Why are those errors occurring? What can we do to eliminate those problems?"

As people become engaged in helping identify waste, you should ask them to *quantify* how much that waste is costing each year. This is a smart idea because you want people to stay focused on the reason you're brainstorming waste; this is your first step in increasing net profits by 5 percent over last year. In order to know if you've made an effective overall plan to do that, you have to know how much each initiative will help your profits.

Once you have guided your executive team in identifying a significant amount of areas of waste, you can guide them in prioritizing them from biggest waste areas to smallest. Then take the top five (for example), and one by one, ask your executive team specifically what needs to happen in order to stop that waste and save money (increase profits). The solutions they give will lead you directly to the necessary *action steps* people need to execute in order to solve the problems and move you toward your objective (in this example, raising profits by 5 percent over last year).

For example, let's say one of the areas that your executive team identified as being an area of waste is in "serving unprofitable customers; customers that demand you offer the lowest price while being one of your most high-maintenance customers." (You know the ones, don't you? They're the accounts you actually lose money servicing!)

Let's say that during your possible solutions phase of the meeting, your production manager suggests, "We need to increase Customer X's pricing so we can make money, or we simply need to be okay with losing their business." If the team agrees to this solution, then the action step is clear: The sales manager (or chief estimator) gets the action step of instructing the people who prepare the quotes that we are no longer going to provide discounts to Customer X. The sales manager then becomes responsible for making sure his staff executes this order. And that's how problems are solved! Step by step, one action step at a time.

To continue with this example, let's presume the controller discovered another area of waste: "We don't competitively bid our purchases enough. I see a lot of purchases every month—significant ones—that don't even have purchase orders attached. I think we spend too much money for the things we buy, and I think we have a tendency to overpurchase since so many people are allowed to make purchases without getting approval."

From that suggestion, at least a couple ideas will be generated to eliminate this area of waste. For example, the team could decide to institute a policy that "purchases over $500 require three competitive bids attached to the purchase order" and that "all purchases require purchase orders from now on." Then the team (or the CEO) determines who is in the best position to carry out this solution. In this example, the CEO may say to his controller, "Carol, please make sure the team knows our new procedures relative to purchasing. All purchases require POs from now on, and all purchases over $500 require three competitive bids." Now Carol knows that she's responsible for making it happen!

And this process continues until the end of the meeting.

Then, as soon as practical after the meeting (no more than twenty-four hours), the notes of what was discussed and the specific action steps that came from the discussion are typed and distributed to all the executive team members. This makes it possible for everyone to remember what they worked on and what they're each responsible for completing. For accountability reasons, it is critically important that the person who is responsible for ensuring the action step is completed is listed by name in the notes. Using the above examples, the notes would look like the "Sample Executive Team Meeting Notes" which follow:

SAMPLE EXECUTIVE TEAM MEETING NOTES

Executive Team Meeting
March 31 Notes
Goal: Increase profit margin by 5% over last year.
Strategy #1: Eliminate waste.
Action Steps

1. Jim (estimating manager): Instruct the estimating department that effective immediately, Customer X can only be quoted using standard pricing, no discounts whatsoever. Please explain to the estimators that our objective is to increase our profit margin by 5 percent over last year, and "reducing waste" is the strategy we're focusing on now to help us achieve that goal. Let them know that last year, we lost an estimated $3,700 from serving Customer X and we either need to turn this into a profitable relationship, or we need to walk away from Customer X so we don't continue to lose this money.

2.   Carol (controller): Please draft and distribute a memo to the entire team stating that effective immediately, all purchases require a purchase order in advance of making a purchase and that you will not authorize payment without one. Also, please include in that memo that effective immediately, all purchases $500 and over require three competitive bids and that each bid must be stapled to the purchase order when submitted. Please explain in this memo why we're instituting this policy: Let the team know that our objective is to increase our profit margin by 5 percent over last year, and reducing waste is the strategy we're focusing on now to be able to achieve that goal. Let them know that at our exec team meeting, we projected that with competitive bidding and better purchasing controls; we estimated that we can add $8,750 to our bottom line this year over last.

In actuality, the notes from this executive team meeting will be longer than the example just provided. Typically, there will be more than just a couple of action steps that come from these meetings. But the notes should follow the format of the sample notes: (1) date of meeting, (2) goal (objective), (3) strategy, (4) action steps assigned to individual executive team members with (5) reasons for the action step, and (6) if practical, a specific estimated outcome from the initiative.

Why do you think it's important for your executive team to explain to their people why the action steps were planned and what the expected impact (benefit) of that action step is projected to be?

When everyone understands *why* you're doing something, a couple things happen. First, your team will support your plans because they see the value in it. People don't like change for changes' sake, but they do appreciate smart change for improvements' sake. Second, this is a great way to get every brain in the game! Here's a fact: the executive team has limitations too. By getting your entire team involved in reaching your goals, you'll have more ideas to choose from, better ideas, and you'll have an entire team of people more engaged in reaching your goals. This helps you for obvious reasons, but it also helps your individual employees. When people are more informed and have the opportunity to make suggestions, they feel more respected and valued. Who do you think make better employees, people that don't feel valued and respected or those that do? I know the answer is obvious, but sometimes we forget that during the day; we need to remember!

The notes from the executive team meeting are important to remind people what they're doing, why they're doing it, and who's responsible for executing each individual action step. But the notes have another critically important value: they are used as an accountability tool at the next meeting!

At the next executive team meeting–the one after our example meeting–the CEO would start the meeting by reminding everyone what the goal is: Increase profits by 5 percent over last year. He would remind everyone what strategy is being worked on to meet that goal: Reduce waste. Then, he would go through the action steps from last month, one by one, to ensure they were executed.

In this example, he would read action step one from the prior month's notes and then say, "Jim, how'd it go?" Jim would respond that it went well and everyone's on board. The CEO would then ask, "Do you still think this is the right way to go?" If Jim answered, "Yes," then the CEO would say something like this: "Okay, good. Can we just give you the action step of checking on the next couple quotes to Customer X and report back to the executive team whether this price increase was accepted or rejected by Customer X? That way, we can better measure the impact on profitability. Either we'll lose Customer X and save the money we used to lose on them, or we'll keep them with higher pricing and we can add our new profit on top of the amount we used to lose to determine a more accurate projected benefit from this initiative." Jim would say, "Sure, I'll do that." And then, that action step becomes action step number one in the new month's notes.

Then, the CEO would read action step two and ask Carol if she completed her action step and if she has any other feedback about that. Then, the CEO might ask Carol if she would report back to the team next month if anyone is failing to follow the new procedures. Carol would say yes, and that would become action step number two in this month's notes.

And this continues all the way through each action step of the prior month. Sometimes (as in the examples above), action steps build onto themselves and lead to subsequent action steps. Other times, the verification that the action step was completed constitutes the end. From the example above, in the following month's executive team meeting, Jim would report back that Company X had either accepted the new, higher pricing or he would report back that Company X rejected the higher pricing and took their business elsewhere. Either of those scenarios is fine with the executive team, so there would be no further action step on that tactic. That plan is complete.

Here's an example of when the completion of the action step does not constitute the plan being complete: Let's say at the following executive team meeting, the estimating manager (Jim) said to the team, "Our new procedure to require three competitive bids for all purchases over $500 isn't working out so well. Our estimators are putting in a lot of extra time to secure three bids and the difference between the highest bid and the lowest bid is always within $15, but it's taking hours of labor to create requests for quote, review the bids, and notify the bidders who won. Furthermore, we're generally getting one or two quotes back quickly, but we rarely get all three bids back quickly. This causes us delays in our ability to get work into production and is putting our own client deadlines in jeopardy."

The CEO may say, "Those are great points, Jim." Then the CEO may turn to the executive team and say, "What do you think we ought to do?"

One of the executives may respond, "What if we raise the limit to $1,000 instead of $500? Would it be worth it then?" Or someone else may respond, "Why don't we stick with our original plan of asking for three quotes for all purchases over $500, but put time limits on receiving the quotes back from our vendors. Give them four hours to turnaround the quote. Then, in four hours, you can decide which vendor to use based on who has provided you the best quote in the allotted time. If only one returned the quote on time, then that company gets our business." Or someone else may respond, "I think we should ask for three quotes, but we should give the ability to make a purchase after the first two quotes come in."

There are many different ideas on how to adjust the original plan. The important thing is that you adjust your plans as new challenges arise. And then, give action steps to execute those adjusted plans.

From the hypothetical executive team's work we've been discussing, you can see that the executive team *planned* when they were brainstorming ways to reduce waste and then they created specific action steps to be taken in order to fulfill their plans. Then, between meetings, the team *executed* the action steps. At the next meeting, they *measured* the success (e.g., made sure the action steps were executed and got feedback on how they went). If the execution phase was successful as planned, there would be no need to adjust their original plans. But if the measuring process presented challenges to the original plans, *adjustments* would be made to those plans and then the new adjusted plans would be executed.

The key to successful business improvement is (1) to plan effectively, then (2) execute vigorously, then (3) measure periodically, and (4) adjust accordingly; and then continue this cycle again by executing the new adjusted plans. At your first (or your next) executive team meeting, please explain this to your executive team so everyone's clear on the executive team's purpose. Specifically, let them know that their job is to identify opportunities (problems), plan to solve them, oversee the execution of the plans, measure the results generated from executing the plans, and if necessary, adjust the plans and then oversee the execution of those new adjusted plans.

Your executive team is essential in being able to formulate the best plans. The executive team helps you put overall plans into specific action steps. Then, your executive team is responsible and accountable to ensure the action steps are completed. Since your executive team members are on the frontline or have easy access to the frontline, your executive team will be able to more easily measure the results of all the action steps. Finally, when plans need to be adjusted, you'll have every brain in the game and can come up with the smartest, most efficient way to adjust your original plan and then move that new plan back into the execution phase.

Now, let's go back to the illustrations at the beginning of this white paper. Can you imagine the business owner on the left trying to brainstorm a plan, oversee the execution of those plans, measure the results, adjust the plans, and then go back into overseeing execution all by him or herself? There's just no way.

On the other hand, if plans are not being made, executed, measured, and adjusted regularly, then what happens to a company? It begins to tip and money, opportunity, and value are sacrificed!

Perhaps the single most important thing for business owners to do is to create a smart and functioning executive team. This will make your company more profitable and more valuable. It will allow people in your company the opportunity for professional growth and personal fulfillment. And finally, it will allow you, the owner, to be able to have much more control, balance, peace, and happiness in your business and in your life.

REVIEW / ACTION STEPS

1. If you don't already have an executive team at your company, it's time to create one! Think of each person on your team that leads a department or division. This could include your sales manager, production manager, controller, customer service manager, store manager, office manager, general manager, HR manager, IT manager, any person that oversees a particular department, division, or location in your business. If you only employ a few people, you may choose to have your top person or maybe even everyone on your team to be on your executive team. The important thing is that you're bringing people onto your executive team that are capable of helping you work on the business and who will either execute the action steps you come up with themselves or

oversee the execution of these action steps with the people in their chains of command.

2. Decide on a regularly scheduled day/time to have your executive team meetings. (For example, the first Tuesday of each month from 6:00 p.m. to 8:00 p.m.) Let everyone on the exec team know the schedule and ask them to plan around it because their attendance is required.

3. Have each person on your new (or existing) executive team create a "master list" of all of the opportunities, problems, and challenges they see in the business. (Note: Please see White Paper 2 to learn about creating an Opportunities List.) Ask your executive team members to make a list of all of the objectives your company should focus on achieving. Have them bring this list to your first (or next) executive team meeting. You may want to suggest they consider:

- Increasing profits
- Decreasing expenses
- Improving customer service
- Improving employee retention
- Improving customer retention
- Improving your sales / marketing efforts
- Improving your efficiencies
- Reducing your labor costs
- Improving the company culture (morale)

- Expanding into a new market (geographically or in product/service offerings)
- Dealing with employee issues
- Filling a position that's been open for too long
- Improving quality
- Improving inventory turn or speed of delivery
- Creating a second (or third) shift
- Etc.

4. At your first (or next) executive team meeting, have everyone go through their list. As they're reading their lists, write down the ideas that should go on your company's Opportunities List. (This is the master listing of all the things standing in the way from where your company is today to where you'd like it to be.) By the end of this first meeting, you should have an agreed-upon master list (Opportunities List) of all of the areas in the business that your executive team will focus on to work toward your goals. By the time this meeting ends, your list should be prioritized. (See 5 below.)

5. From your Opportunities List, choose the top three to five ideas (initiatives) you want to focus on first and then start working through them one by one. Follow the same type of model as the example provided in the white paper above.

In the example, the executive team was focused on increasing their profit margin by 5 percent over last year, first, by focusing on where money is currently being wasted.

6. Continue with your regularly scheduled executive team meetings. Remember that the executive team's job is to (1) plan how to capitalize on opportunities or solve your existing problems, (2) execute or oversee the execution of the plans, (3) measure the results of your executed plans, (4) adjust your plans as necessary and go back into execution with new or continued action steps. This is a never-ending process, so please be sure to keep your scheduled meetings.

7. Be sure to provide your executive team members the notes from each meeting along with a listing of the action steps that were agreed to. These notes should be provided as soon as practical but no more than twenty-four hours after each executive team meeting. Please don't skip this step! The notes are a great accountability tool, and they also help everyone stay focused on achieving your goals. Without written notes, it becomes too easy for initiatives to simply fall by the wayside.

8. Finally, be sure you're building a culture of accountability by staying regimented and disciplined during your meetings and ensuring that all action steps are assigned, completed appropriately, and on time. Your executive team

needs to understand that it is not okay to be late or to be sloppy with action steps. The "tail follows the head." In other words, your team will follow the leaders. If your leaders set the example and meet their obligations, then you should expect that your team will do the same.

SUMMARY

Through years of experience in working with business owners, it's become clear to me that the difference between companies that can execute and companies that can't boils down to one primary reason: Companies that execute have a *team* of people engaged in moving the ball. Companies that get stuck are led by CEOs that allow their companies to become too dependent on a single person—the owner—to make all the plans, solve all the problems, oversee all initiatives, and correct challenges without the help of others. That concentrated command and control simply makes it impossible for a business to meet its true potential.

In his book *Winning*, Jack Welch talks about the importance of getting "every brain in the game." In the book *Execution*, written by Ram Charan and Larry Bossidy, you can read about the strategy process, the people process, and the operations process, all of which depend on a team of dedicated people to execute the plans.

If you feel stuck, if you feel trapped by your business, if you see an opportunity but don't have the time or ability to capitalize on that opportunity, then it's very likely you're trying to do too much yourself.

As business owners, we tend to think we're the smartest people in the room. We think we're the best person or only person that can come up with the best solutions. That's simply not the case unless you've done a poor job hiring your employees.

You can benefit tremendously by getting ideas from your people. You can effectively oversee initiatives with the assistance of others. It's extremely difficult—even impossible—to be able to measure and adjust your own plans in a timely manner. But with an executive team, this is not only achievable, it is expected.

Your plans will be smarter. Your execution will be stronger. Your measurements and adjustments will be faster. And all the while you're benefitting from this, you're simultaneously creating an environment where your team members will benefit from their own personal and professional development. Everyone wins!

Your regularly scheduled executive team meetings also serve as a powerful "accountability forum." Without accountability, plans may get drawn up, but they may not be executed. Or at best, they get executed, but never measured and adjusted. Talk about spinning your wheels!

If you haven't read the book *The E-Myth Revisited* by Michael Gerber yet, you really need to do that. I'm also strongly recommending you read *Winning* by Jack Welch and *Execution* by Charan and Bossidy. These books will expand your understanding and enhance your ability to get things done. In fact, the smartest

CEO will also buy those books for his or her executive team members and give them the action steps to read those books as well.

There's nothing magical about planning, executing, measuring, and adjusting. It just needs to happen regularly with a team of dedicated leaders. Get the pressure off your own back. The other leaders in your company want to share in that responsibility! They want to help you and they want to make their company (which you own) the most profitable, successful, valuable company they can create. Give them that opportunity, and give your company the ability to grow larger than you alone.

Nothing worthwhile is easy or fast. It will require focus, determination, and commitment. But you can do it!

Go get unstuck!

STRATEGY 4

EVERY BRAIN IN THE GAME

Remember the "early days" of your business? Everyone on your team wore different hats because you couldn't afford to hire specialists. You all worked hard. You all put your hearts and souls into making the business succeed. Everyone thought of it as "their" company, even though most didn't have any shares of company stock.

The furniture was ugly and old. The office space was cramped and smelled moldy. Your rented office copier was constantly jamming. Your Web site was "under construction" for almost a year! Remember payday? You started the day asking, "Who really needs their check today and who can wait until Monday or Tuesday?" "Do you really need your car allowance check, or can it wait a few more days?"

Even though the pay was low and the hours were long, everyone had passion in their work. You worked in harmony. The bonds of friendship were glued. You were all doing battle together. Those truly were the "good 'ol days!"

Years have passed. Your start-up team is still there, now in high-level positions. None of your employees are required to work excessive overtime anymore. Everyone earns much more than in the early days. The benefits are better; there's more vacation time. The company's survival is no longer threatened as it was your first couple of years in business. Oh, and your Web site even won an award!

But things don't feel the same. As you've added new employees over the years, the once dynamic "Whatever It Takes" culture has faded. Your old war dogs that sweated with you in the early days have lost their fire. The new cadre of employees just doesn't understand that their job description also includes doing anything and everything they can do to serve your company and your clients better. The tightness of your team has been replaced with cliques, gossip, and backstabbing.

You've held staff meetings. You've begged your leaders to help you get things back to the way they used to be. You even had a company party. But nothing has worked.

Face it, even you are affected. You used to do twice as much work in half the time. You used to have goals, fueled with passion. But now, you've settled into mediocrity.

You have a gnawing feeling in your gut, though. You know the culture isn't what it should be and you wish things were different. You wish you and your team had that passion again. You wish your work had the meaning it once did. But you don't know what to do to get it back and you're not even sure you have the energy to try any more.

Jack Welch (former chairman of General Electric) said, "You pay a person for his or her hands, but they'll give you their brains and their hearts for free. All you have to do is ask!"

When's the last time you asked your employees for their opinions? Do you know how they feel about the current corporate culture? Do you know what they love about their work or hate about their jobs? Do you know what they would change about your company if they had the power to? Do you know what their goals are? Do they know what your goals are? Does anyone know what your company goals are?

Does anyone know what's costing your company profits, profit margin, new customers, repeat business, and employee retention? What does your team think about their current compensation plans? What's more important to them: increased health benefits, more time off, dress-down days, free lunches once in a while, or increased pay? Do they know what needs to be accomplished in order for them to realize these added benefits?

Why are their cliques? Does your team trust you? Do they trust the middle managers? Do they think of their current employment as a career or just a job until something better comes along?

The best way to find out is to ask! Just ask them!

Like all aspects of developing your business, building a strong corporate culture can't happen overnight and it won't happen on its own. You can't conquer the world in one fell swoop, but you can take deliberate calculated action steps on a daily basis to get you from where you are now to where you want to be.

How about this for a first step: Create your own Team Member Evaluation. This doesn't need to be scientific. Just think of all the questions you have about your team's perceptions. What would you like to know from your team? Write down all the questions you have for them and then put it in a Word document.

Make sure your team knows what you intend to do with the feedback they give you. Make sure everyone knows that you want their "honest" opinions and that you won't try to figure out who wrote the evaluations if people choose to keep their opinions anonymous. They should not feel threatened in any way. Remind them that in order for things to improve, you need the straight scoop on what the biggest issues are. Also remind your team that gossiping and complaining will not improve things, but candid feedback with suggested solutions can be step 1 in the process of building an excellent place to work.

Once you have this valuable information, you're well on your way, but the real power comes from how you use this information.

To get started, compile the survey responses so you and your executive team can clearly see all of the answers that were given to each question and then prepare a full report for your team where you will:

1. Provide a copy of all of the answers that were given for each question.

2. Write a thoughtful reply to each answer.

3. Let the team know what action steps are being formulated to address the points that make sense to address.

4. Provide the deadlines you've set for completing those action steps.

5. Provide the date you'll send out a follow-up survey.

Let's review each of those points:

1. Provide a copy of all of the answers that were given for each question.

   All you have to do is create a document listing each question, and under each question, type in each response to that question. To keep it authentic, I suggest you do not edit the answers; do not fix typos, do not fix misspellings, grammatical mistakes, or anything else. Instead, write it as it was written. The only exception to this is if you believe that censoring an answer is necessary to protect someone's feelings (not the owner's feelings, but another team member's). You do not want anyone to be publically humiliated. Provide as much of the answer as you can, but please protect people from being embarrassed by name (unless it is the owner).

2. Write a thoughtful reply to each answer.

   Absolute humility, candor, and curiosity are a must! You and your executive team may be insulted or hurt by a particular answer (or answers). Please humble yourselves because the point may be valid. Take the time to thoughtfully consider why that person may have written the answer that hurt your feelings. If after consideration you determine that the person has a point, admit it in your reply! It's okay that you're not perfect. It's admirable that you admit it when you see your own shortcomings. In your reply, you can even say that it hurt your feelings, but you see the point and appreciate that this point was made. The more candid you are, the better.

Other answers you will simply not agree with at all. Take this as a teachable moment. In your reply, explain to everyone why (specifically) you do not agree with what was stated. Beware that you don't do this in a confrontational manner! That would be a big mistake. Instead, respectfully and specifically state your rationale for not agreeing with them. Remember, be constructive and instructive, not judgmental!

Other answers will include good ideas you hadn't thought of before or that you haven't acted on yet. They aren't emotional; they're just sound, tactical (or strategic) ideas. These are easy to reply to: Simply thank the person and let them know it's a great idea!

3. Let the team know what action steps are being formulated to address the points that make sense to address.

When a team member makes a valid point, then something needs to happen in order to fix the problem or meet the opportunity being sought. In this section of the Full Report, explain specifically what action steps you have assigned to yourself, your executive team, or your individual team members to begin the process of getting things the way they should be. Be specific! This is an incredibly important step to give yourself credibility because asking for answers to your questions is great, but committing to do something specific based on the answers is demonstrating strong leadership. After all, nothing happens without action! Please make sure you have action steps to take advantage of every good idea presented to you. If you can't address it quite yet (due to higher priority initiatives), simply give yourself the action step of revisiting this on a particular date (and be sure you stick with it, they're watching!).

4. Provide the deadlines you've set for completing those action steps.

   To say you're committed to doing something (an action step) is fine, but without providing a deadline for completion, you aren't really committed at all. You're hopeful, but not committed. People want and deserve to know what you're going to do (the action step) and also when you'll do it (the deadline). In doing this, you're leading by example in building on your culture of accountability.

5. Provide the date you'll send out a follow-up survey.

A follow-up survey is a survey you'll put out at a later date to get your team's feedback on how things are progressing since the Full Report was issued. You'll ask if the action steps promised were completed on time. You'll ask if the leadership team (or you, the owner) have done a great, fair, or poor job in making improvements that were identified in the initial survey. You'll allow your team to openly and candidly evaluate *your* performance!

If your first reaction to this is that you're the owner and that you are not accountable to the people you pay, then I suggest you find a great book on leadership and dig in because you have much to learn. "Leadership by example" is just under "integrity" as the top attributes of a leader. You expect your team to deliver on their promises, so you must also. You expect your team to be accountable, so you must also. You will be highly respected when you lead this way.

Please use your follow-up survey as an opportunity to ask any new questions you may have that were not asked in the initial survey. You may even want to repeat some of the questions that were in the initial survey to see if people are thinking differently now. When you ask a new series of questions (or repeat questions), you'll get new answers that will allow you and your executive team to consider, then reply to, then act on, and get results from. This puts you in a perpetual mode of asking questions, getting answers, replying to the answers, acting on good ideas, and leading by example in holding yourself accountable.

This isn't going to be easy, but it will work. Remember, "People don't care how much you know until they know how much you care." When you presented them the opportunity to speak freely via the anonymous survey, you demonstrated that you care.

Then, you showed them respect again by replying to their answers via the Full Report. You told them what actions would be taken based on their suggestions and you told them when they should expect results. Then, you followed up to get their suggestions on how well you did with their initial suggestions! Now that is fantastic leadership and your people will certainly know how much you care. They will return the favor!

It's not easy, but it can be fun, and when the passion is reignited, you'll know it was worth the effort.

I wish you my best in getting unstuck!

REVIEW / ACTION STEPS

1. Create your own team-member questionnaire: To do this, write down all the questions you have about your team's perceptions. What do you want to know from your team members? Here are some sample questions that were mentioned in the white paper above. Please consider these

to get you going in creating your own team-member survey, or just go ahead and create your own questions:

Sample Questions from White Paper

- How do you feel about our corporate culture?
- What do you love about your job?
- What do you love about our company?
- What do you dislike about your job?
- What do you dislike about our company?
- If you could change anything at our company, what would it be and how would you do it?
- What are your personal goals?
- What do you think my personal goals are (the owner's)?
- What are our company goals?
- What's costing our company profits or profit margin?
- What do our customers love about us?
- What do our customers not love about us?
- Why do employees leave (our company)?
- Do you get thanked enough for your contributions?
- What's most important to you (circle only one, please): increased health benefits, more vacation days, dress-down days,

our company expanding and therefore providing more opportunity for professional development, pay raises, or add your own in the space provided_____.

- What do you think we need to accomplish in order for these perks (written above) to be implemented?

- Are their cliques here at (your company), or do we operate in total unity?

- Do you trust your teammates?

- Do you trust me (the owner)?

- Do you trust your immediate supervisor?

- Do you think of your employment here as a potential career or just a job until something better comes along?

Again, the list is as long as your curiosity allows! As you create your team-member survey, please only ask the questions you're sincerely interested in knowing the answers to.

2. Create a cover letter that will accompany your team-member survey. To help you in creating this, here is an example of a cover letter that you can modify if it will help you:

Sample Team Member Survey Cover Letter

Dear Team,
    Please find a team survey attached to this letter.

The purpose of this survey is to find out what each member of this team thinks about different aspects of our business and your employment at (our company). When we get the results of your surveys, we will provide you a copy of how each question was answered by everyone that participated!

With the information you provide, the Executive Team at (our company) is going to determine the different areas of opportunity we have to improve our business. We are also going to learn where we need to make changes in order to better serve our team.

The answers you provide will be taken seriously and I am personally asking that you please answer these questions with complete thoughtfulness and honesty, otherwise, this is just a waste of time. This is an anonymous survey and we ask that you please *do not* put your names on the surveys. I assure you there will be absolutely no effort to try to figure out who wrote the responses no matter how disappointing we may find some of the answers. We want the straight scoop, and by keeping this anonymous, everyone should feel comfortable providing your true thoughts and opinions we're asking for in this survey.

Once you complete the survey, please seal it in the provided envelope and slide it under my door or put it in my mailbox in the break room. I am not going to open any of the submissions until June 1.

I am requesting that you return the completed survey no later than May 31 at 5:00 p.m.

No later than June 20, I will provide each of you a full report from this survey, including everyone's different answers to each question. Next to each of your responses, our executive team will address each of your points. We'll let you know what we think about your answer or comment and what (if anything) we intend to do about it. By providing this full report, you'll know where the (company name) leadership team stands relative to your opinions and you can hold the leadership team accountable to delivering on our promises for change that will be stated in the full report.

Thank you in advance for your candid feedback. You're valued and appreciated more than I can tell you.

If you don't want to participate in this survey, simply slide this blank form under my door or in my mailbox in the break room. I only want you to participate in this if you want to and if you're committed to doing your best job on it! I hope you participate and take full advantage of this opportunity to be heard. We can't fix things if we don't know they're broken. We're counting on everyone to help us make things better here at (your company). Thank you!

Sincerely yours,
(your name)

3. Once you and your executive team have gone through the survey results, please create a full report for your team. Remind them of the questions and then provide them everyone's

anonymous answers to each of the questions so people can (1) see their own answers and know that you considered them and (2) so people can learn what other people on the team think about things. Be sure to include your candid response to every answer that was provided. This report should also include a listing of "action steps" that you and your executive team are going to take to address each of the issues and also include the deadline for completing the action steps. If the suggestion is good, but low priority, be sure you give the action step to revisit that suggestion by a certain date. For any issues or suggestions made that you're not going to act on, please address those in the full report by letting everyone know why you're not going to address those particular issues at this time (or ever). Don't be judgmental or confrontational, but do be candid.

4. Make sure you and your executive team live up to the promises you made in the full report! If you don't, you'll lose credibility with your team. You'll also miss a huge opportunity to improve your company. If you're keeping an Opportunities List (discussed in detail in Strategy 2), add these initiatives to that list and work vigorously as an executive team to turn those opportunities into tangible results.

5. Once your executive team has made progress completing initiatives that were generated from the original team member questionnaire, provide a follow-up survey to your team. Here

is an example of a follow-up survey that you can use to help you create your own:

Sample Team Member Follow-Up Survey

Dear Team,

Back in May of this year, we performed a team member survey. The full report from this survey was issued to the team on June 19.

As I've previously stated, the results of this survey was eye-opening for me, to say the least. Our Executive Team and I took the responses seriously and spent much time considering, discussing, and researching the information you provided.

We met for several hours over the course of two weeks to formulate a plan to address the issues that had been expressed.

We executed this plan the best way we knew how and I believe all of the commitments made in the Full Report were fulfilled.

As we approach the four-month mark of initiating our plan, I am now requesting your candid (honest) feedback regarding the changes that have taken place.

For the team members that have been with (our company) for less than four months or so, you can't know firsthand of the effects of these changes. Therefore, I am simply asking you to fill out the questions you believe you have enough knowledge to answer.

Please take this questionnaire seriously as your answers will be addressed seriously.

Please *do not* place your name on this survey! I want you to be as comfortable as possible in being completely truthful.

It is entirely your decision whether or not to participate in this survey, but I hope you do. It would truly be a shame if you missed an opportunity such as this to be heard. (Our company) is much bigger than any one person. Everyone at (our company) matters. I am humbly asking that you take some time to let your thoughts, feelings, and ideas come to light.

Please place your completed survey either in my mailbox (in the break room) or slide under my door no later than Monday, October 5!

Thank you.

—(CEO)

Questionnaire

1. Do you believe that the senior leadership at (our company) was serious about addressing the issues brought forth in the last Team Member Survey? YES or NO

2. Do you believe that the tactics that our executive team planned were appropriate (smart)? YES or NO (If tactics were not smart, what should we have done differently?) _____

_____

_____

_____

_____.

3. Has the executive team done a great job, a decent job, or a poor job in executing the plan that was communicated to the team via the Team Member Survey Full Report (back in June)? Please circle one: GREAT JOB DECENT JOB POOR JOB

4. What plans has the executive team failed to deliver on? Please describe: _____

   _____

   _____

   _____

   _____.

5. How do you view the corporate culture at (our company) today? Please circle one: FANTASTIC DECENT POOR

6. If I could change anything at (our company), I would: _____

   _____

   _____

   _____

   _____.

7. How confident are you that our current leadership team can continue to lead our company into the future? Please circle one: VERY CONFIDENT CONFIDENT NOT CONFIDENT

8. From mid-2008 through early 2012, (company) profits were significantly dampened by the economy. We had several clients go out of business due to bankruptcy;

that caused us to lose those customers, but also left us holding the bag for over $160,000 in money that was owed to us that we'll never be able to collect. Despite that, we've continued to grow. It appears the worst is over (universe willing!). As I begin preparing our operating budget for next year, I am going to have some aggressive profit projections! Here's the question for you:

If / when (our company) gets back to hitting our profit goals, the biggest benefit I would like to see (our company) offer is: (please select only one)

a. Provide 100% health insurance coverage (instead of the 50% currently offered).

b. Offer matching contributions in our 401K.

c. Put the money into bigger pay raises for those who earn it.

d. Make larger prizes for "The Annual Bonus Game."

e. Open a new location sooner rather than later.

f. _____
(write it in!)

g. The thing I like best about my immediate supervisor is: _____

_____

_____

_____

_____.

9. The thing I like least about my immediate supervisor is: _____

_____

_____

_____

_____.

10. To me, my employment at (our company) is (please circle one)

A CAREER A JOB I ENJOY FOR NOW JUST A PAYCHECK

End of survey... Thank you!

6. Repeat the process. Provide a full report of the follow-up survey and what you and your executive team intend to do with the results. Periodic employee (or team member) surveys can be a terrific tool for you to use as you strive to keep your team engaged in the business. It will also give you critical information coming from your frontline that will be valuable in knowing what to do next to build the profitability and value of your company. Remember, none of this is rocket science. Just ask the questions you want to know the answers to, and everything else will fall into place as long as you act on the results of the survey.

SUMMARY

When you get to the office each morning, you should be greeted with a feeling of exhilaration by your individual team members. Likewise, you should feel exhilarated as well. The only way that's possible is if people, including you, want to be there.

When people are comfortable, they can give their best efforts. When comfort is replaced by uncertainty, distrust, cliques, politics, and all the other garbage that we should have outgrown by eighth grade, then production suffers and so does your company's ability to wow your clients. Collectively, poor company cultures costs untold millions of dollars each year to companies that don't pay attention to it.

Your questionnaire will be a great step in getting everything out on the table so you know what you must address.

When you take the idea of getting every brain in the game to all levels in your organization, you're maximizing your ability to hear the real deal. At the same time, you give all of your team members dignity, first, by asking them what they think, and then secondly, by providing a full report explaining to them either why you did or did not accept their recommendations.

You can't push a rope. Similarly, you can't push people to give you their best when the culture is not where it needs to be.

If you want to learn more about the benefits of building a strong culture at your company, I strongly suggest you read *Gung Ho* by Ken Blanchard and

Sheldon Bowles. It's a quick, easy, fun read, and the content of the book is fantastic!

Remember, conducting the survey is not an end in and of itself. You need to address every single idea, suggestion, and opinion that is submitted and you need to do it with dignity and honesty. Your executive team will be a great asset for you to finalize the questionnaire, execute it, and then make plans to act on the results.

The team member survey can be very powerful. But please be aware that the true power came from responding to the survey first with words, then with action. Conducting an employee survey and doing nothing tangible with the results is not only a waste of time; it will dishearten your team members that put thoughtful effort into filling out the surveys. You must be committed to solving the issues!

This is not a quick, easy solution. But this will work if you do it right and follow up with vigor.

Go get unstuck!

STRATEGY 5

PEOPLE PROBLEMS

A company is not just bricks and mortar. It's not just a name. It's not just a product or service. The biggest determinate in a business' personality (and ultimately, its success or failure) is *people*.

Why, then, do business owners allow people problems to go unaddressed?

Before we answer that, let's explore some typical people problems that surround us in our companies. Here's a shortlist:

- A salesperson that doesn't bring in new business.

- A person who is frequently late, sick, or leaves early.

- The staff member that likes to bring personal drama to work every day.

- Someone with a poor work ethic.

- A person who lies, cheats, or deceives.

- The employee that makes a lot of mistakes, incompetence.

- A selfish person that serves him or herself first, the team second (or worse).

- Someone that resists positive change.

- A person with a bad attitude.

- The happy employee that is always extremely "busy," but doesn't accomplish much that's worthwhile.

- The once fabulous team member that has slipped into mediocrity.

Feel free to take a minute here to add to this list... it's endless! Now ask yourself candidly, "Do we have any of these people problems at (your company)?" It's likely you do! Now ask yourself, "What am I doing about it?" If you're like most business owners, the true answer to that question is either "not much" or "absolutely nothing"; you've just accepted it.

There it is! The biggest mistake business owners make! If you're guilty, please stay with me!

Now, we'll answer the question, "Why do business owners allow people problems to go unaddressed?" How's this for starters:

- No time.

- No energy.

- Too busy.

- The person may quit; besides, nobody's perfect.

- I don't like conflict.

- He/she will only make excuses and be offended, and it won't work anyway.

- I don't want to make waves.

- There are a lot of great traits the person has; I don't want to be too critical.

- I'm loyal to my people for better or for worse.

- If I ask that person to improve, he/she will want me to improve on my weaknesses too.

The complete list of answers to why people don't address people problems is just as long as the list of problems people have…it's endless! Now ask yourself, "Why aren't *you* addressing the specific people problems you have at your company?"

If you answered the questions above candidly, you may be starting to squirm in your seat right now. You may be tempted to make the conscious decision to stop reading this, stop thinking about this and bury your head back in the proverbial sand. Here's a shortlist of why you shouldn't do that:

- It's costing your company money.

- It's killing the morale of the very best people on your team.

- Your customers are either directly or indirectly suffering.

- Your business is not as valuable as it could be.

- You're losing growth opportunities.

- You're personally suffering from stress and frustration caused by poor performers.

- You're robbing the poor performer of a personal and/or professional growth opportunity.

- You're making your own life more complicated than it needs to be.

I encourage you to go ahead and take my next statement personally: If you, the business owner, aren't addressing the people problems in your company, then *you* are a people problem. Please read that last sentence again; it's very important. "If you aren't addressing the people problems in your company, then *you* are a people problem!"

If my candor has ticked you off, I'm sorry. The intention of my honest feedback isn't to hurt your feelings; it's meant to be constructive. I want to help you help yourself, which in turn will allow you to help your own company.

If you're still reading, then you probably see the incredible benefits of addressing people problems. Maybe you're hoping for a suggestion to get you into action. If so, here it is:

Schedule a time to meet with your problem person. When the time comes, start your meeting by telling the person that you're going to have an honest adult conversation with him or her. Let that person know that your intention isn't to hurt his feelings; it's meant to be constructive. You want to help that person help himself, which in turn will allow him to be more valuable to your business. (Sound familiar? Go up two paragraphs and read it!)

Then, give it to him straight! As unemotionally as you can, let him know the real deal. Take your time. Be specific. Don't allow things to get out of hand; remember the goal isn't to prove someone guilty, it's to help that person see what you see and then to agree on specific actions to start down the road to improvement.

Don't allow this meeting to end until you're both on the same page relative to:

- The specific problem(s).
- The ramifications of those problems on that person's career, your company, your customers, etc.
- The expectations moving ahead.
- The precise action steps required of that person (and perhaps even of you) to alleviate the problems.
- A written commitment from each of you to follow-through on your specific action steps.
- An agreed upon date to meet together again to check progress.

Sounds like an employee review, doesn't it? That's exactly what it is...sort of!

I'm not talking about the typical, useless dog-and-pony shows that many people call reviews. I'm talking about a true, meaningful, constructive conversation that will help everyone and your company become more successful. Unlike a generic employee review, this isn't an event. This is the *beginning* of a process that will require constant follow-up.

Without follow-up and follow-through, nothing really changes. An annual performance review, even a great one, is *transactional* in nature, not *transformational*. Everyone knows that lasting change only happens when there's transformation.

You have to invest time, effort, and energy into this. I know that sounds draining, but when you do it right, you'll see the results. When you see the positive results, you'll find a renewed energy and happiness. I promise!

Your people are either making or breaking your company. The rewards from developing your team are just too great to ignore. The dangers associated with people problems can be deadly to your business. So stop burying your head in the sand and stop worrying so much. Instead, just start talking candidly about it with the people that need the help.

One last offer of advice: Do your best to develop your individual team members, but at some point, you may simply need to cut your losses. In other words, *if you can't change your people, change your people.* Think about that.

It's not easy and it's going to take time, but you can do it.

REVIEW / ACTION STEPS

1. Think about every person on your team and determine where you have people problems. If

you have an executive team, ask each executive team member to do this for the people in their individual chains of command. (And of course, you should determine any executive team members who have developed their own problems.)

2. Prepare for and then have a meeting with your problem person (or people) and make sure you address the following with specifics and detail:

- The specific problem(s).

- The ramifications of those problems on that person's career, your company, your customers, etc.

- The expectations moving ahead.

- The precise action steps required of that person (and perhaps even of you) to alleviate the problems.

- A written commitment from each of you to follow-through on your specific action steps.

- An agreed upon (and scheduled) date to get back together to review progress.

Be sure to follow-up *regularly* to make sure the issues discussed are being addressed properly. Also, be sure you're living up to your end of the bargain. If you had actions steps to help the person, then you must always lead by example and meet your obligations.

You must acknowledge that some people just don't (and won't ever) fit in your company. If you can't change your people's behavior so they are a fit, then you need to change your people for other people who will fit. Remember, a small business can't afford to have even a single weak link. It is ultimately your job to make sure that you and your executive team are fixing people problems quickly and appropriately. It is also your ultimate responsibility to make sure your company is always fielding the best team possible. People problems are way too costly to ignore or to put off until later.

*For more information on how to field the best team you can, read the book *Winning*, by Jack and Suzy Welch. It's a fantastic book that covers a myriad of topics that are important to small business owners (as well as large business owners). An entire chapter of *Winning* is focused on "Differentiation." I think this is a must-read for all business owners. The chapter on "Candor" will make you see honest communication in a whole new light!

SUMMARY

By now, you should be clear on which people problems you have in your company, the negative impact those problems are having on your company, and you should be prepared to face these problems head on.

You know that feeling you get in your gut sometimes when you see someone do something or you hear someone say something that doesn't seem right to you? Well, it's your job to listen to your gut! You have a responsibility to honestly and thoughtfully address things *as they happen* so that little problems don't become big problems.

This takes courage, but as a leader, it's your job to have and to exercise courage.

As you're fixing people problems, please do yourself and everyone else a favor and act more like a "coach" than a "judge." No matter what, you must respect the dignity of the person you're talking to. If you don't, then *you* are a people problem of a different sort!

I'm not suggesting you be weak in your approach, far from it. Hit it straight on and be completely candid; just don't become emotional and don't berate the person.

People problems cost small businesses untold millions of dollars every year. They break the morale of your great people, and they frustrate your customers—possibly to the point of finding a new supplier to replace you.

The emotional drain caused by people problems is substantial. Your people pay for it and so do you.

One final tip regarding your people: Frequently ask yourself, "If I knew then what I know now about this person when I hired him, would I still hire him?" If the answer is no, then you have to ask yourself, "What am I going to do about it?" And then, you have to act.

Remember, as CEO, it's ultimately your job to make sure that you and your managers address people problems immediately. Otherwise, your business will suffer in all the ways we've discussed and your great people will likely run for the hills.

Congratulations on taking the first steps in solving your people problems! It's not going to be easy. It's going to require work and patience, but it will either work or you'll know that it's time to part ways with the problem person. Remember, addressing people problems is not an event. It's something that has to be done real time, every time you see it.

I wish you all the best as you go get unstuck!

STRATEGY 6

PUT YOUR PAYROLL ON A DIET!

For many business owners, payroll is the single highest expense on your income statement. Even businesses that have higher single costs (such as inventory), payroll is always significant.

Oftentimes, we simply accept this expense as a cost of doing business. To a large extent, that's true. However, time and again, business owners compound their own challenges by adding unnecessary "fat" to their payroll.

For example, *are you paying any of your people more than you should for the responsibilities they have?* In other words, do you have people in certain positions earning more than that position warrants?

Here's what happens: As people extend their tenure at our companies, we reward them with pay raises. Many get a pay raise every single year. If people stay in the same position too long, you'll eventually end up paying much more than the position warrants, causing "fat" in your payroll. In addition to putting your company at a competitive disadvantage, you're simultaneously putting those people in danger. In tough economic times or during dips in your business, you'll be forced to look at people's wages and the people who are receiving more than they should will be the first to get canned or have pay cuts forced on them. Either would be a nightmare come true for most people. With proper planning, this nightmare is completely avoidable!

Here's a tip: Make a pay scale for every position in your company. The lowest in the range is for the less experienced new hires. The maximum is the ceiling anyone in that position can earn as base pay. Any additional money paid to employees receiving the maximum for their position will be paid in the form of annual bonuses (or quarterly or monthly, if you prefer). By providing bonus opportunities instead of pay raises, your labor costs become more variable than if you simply give pay raises each year. If times get tough, you can back off on the bonuses without having to give a pay cut. If a seasoned employee has an off-year, you won't have to pay an extraordinarily high rate that is based on longevity and/or past greatness.

Remember, people typically live to their means. They generally don't count on a bonus check to cover their monthly living expenses. But they do count on their base pay. If they don't earn a bonus, they may be disappointed. But if you cut their pay, they may not be able to afford their necessities and they'll most certainly be furious with you.

If you structure pay appropriately, your company has a competitive advantage and your employees are protected. Therefore, your first action step in getting your payroll under control is to *create pay scales for each position in your company.*

Once that's done, you may realize you have a person (or people) already earning more than the ceiling that's appropriate for that position. My suggestion is to bite the bullet. As stated, pay cuts cause anger and hardship. Instead, simply let that person (or people) know that they are currently earning more than the maximum in their job. Let them know that all future additional earnings will come in the form of bonus opportunities. Also, be sure to tell them the reasons for this (you're protecting the business and protecting him / her from future instability).

Here's another question to help you identify payroll fat: *Do you differentiate when giving pay raises?* In other words, does everyone in the same or similar positions get the same amount of pay raise each year, or do some people get more than others because their results are better? I'm hoping your answer is that pay raises are given based strictly on performance, yet I've seen over and again that many business owners sprinkle pay raises equally among their team like snowflakes on a field. If you're an across-the-board, equal-pay-raise type of person, there is little doubt you're intentions are good and you're doing this in the spirit of fairness, but the fact is, this is *unfair* and not good for you, your employees, or your business.

People shouldn't be rewarded simply for showing up. They should be compensated according to the individual results each person brings to the company. When pay raises are distributed equally, the stronger players on your team will rightfully be frustrated that their individual exceptional results are not being acknowledged. Likewise, you're robbing your weaker players of incentive to become better. Think back to high school; How would you have felt if you studied hard and sacrificed in order to earn high grades, but the teacher decided that everyone in the class was going to get an A+ no matter their test scores or homework completion? Would this motivate you to keep studying hard? Of course not! So don't do this now. Don't give pay raises equally. Reward the best people with the highest raises or bonuses.

Here's another simple truth that we sometimes overlook: *People are not entitled to receive pay raises each year.* Yes, you want to reward and retain your great people who bring you the best results and annual pay raises are one way to accomplish that. But the flipping of pages on a calendar does not signify an obligation to give pay raises to everyone.

Many people, including business owners, believe that annual pay raises are necessary. Again, their reasons for this are noble: they think that people should be rewarded for the amount of time they've worked for their employer. But ask yourself this: Would your customers pay you more for your product or service simply because they've been your customer for several years? Would you be okay if one of your vendors charged you more than they charge other customers because you've been their customer for a long time? Then why would you reward an employee simply for being in the job for a long time? I know "cost of living" adjustments can keep things level, but the market is what it is and you have to be conscientious.

My opinion is that if you've had an employee for a long time that hasn't earned an increase in compensation based on his or her individual results, then a pay raise is the last thing you should be giving. Don't give them an extra penny. Instead, provide that person additional training, a candid performance review with specific action steps for improvement, realistic goals, and some coaching. Then hold him/her accountable for the results.

The point is, pay raises and bonuses should never just be *given*. They should be *earned*.

Here's another tip to help you keep your payroll from getting fat: *You don't always have to throw money at people in order to show your appreciation for their hard work and solid results.* Sometimes, just saying thank you is enough! Thanking someone in private will be meaningful and appreciated, but if you thank a person in front of his/her peers, it may even have more power.

Thoughtful and specific handwritten thank-you notes get saved! Why are they saved? Because they're meaningful to the recipient! Don't underestimate the power of a "thank you." Many surveys show that the number one complaint people have about their work is *not* related to their compensation. Instead, it is that nobody thanked them or recognized them for a job well done. I'm guessing you already know this, though. But are you really taking time regularly to thank the folks on your team that deserve it?

There are many other ways to show your appreciation that are less expensive than larger cash bonuses: plaques, trophies, gift certificates, bonus paid days-off, a parking spot, a dress-down day...the list is as long as your mind is creative. Please don't get me wrong: these less expensive tokens of appreciation should *not* substitute financial compensation. People should receive additional money as their performance and results improve. I'm simply suggesting that you mix in some other forms of recognition that may be equally (or more) appreciated by the recipient while also being less costly to you.

When is the last time you looked into reducing your workers' compensation insurance? I'll keep this short and sweet: Just look into it! You may find meaningful savings.

One last quick tip: If you offer health insurance for your team members, you probably competitively shop this each year and look into all the different options available to you. If you haven't, you need to. I'm not suggesting you cut benefits; I'm simply suggesting you make sure you know all your options. Otherwise, a point may come where providing health insurance becomes cost prohibitive to you.

Are you using an employee leasing company to employ your people? There certainly are benefits to some companies in outsourcing employment, but you need to beware! Some leasing companies (many, in fact) charge you workers' compensation rates and other costs that you presume are pass-through costs based on the actual amount the employee leasing company pays on your behalf. Many times, that's simply not true! These may just be additional profit centers that the leasing company benefits from at your expense.

I am not discouraging anyone from utilizing employee leasing, and I am not making an across-the-board claim that all leasing companies follow that practice. I'm simply stating that I know it happens and I'm suggesting you have a competitor (i.e., a payroll processing company or an HR consulting company) conduct an audit for you. It won't cost you much, but could save you plenty! Again, I just want you to explore your options and make the decision that provides you the greatest return on investment with all things being considered.

Remember, every dollar you can reduce in overhead directly impacts your company's bottom line: profits. Labor often accounts for an overwhelmingly significant portion of that overhead. If you can reduce that by even one percentage point, how much additional profit would you realize?

It will take time, effort, and attention to every detail. You'll have to make some gut calls and maybe even make unpopular decisions. But the return on investment could be substantial.

REVIEW / ACTION STEPS

1. Please work with your executive team to create pay scales for each position you employ. You should determine the entry-level pay rate for each position and a corresponding maximum pay-level. There are companies (i.e., employment agencies, HR consulting companies, etc.) that can provide database resources in assisting you

to determine these different pay levels if you want outside help.

2. Please work with your executive team to determine how and when to give pay raises. Pay raises should be merit-based and subjective (not standard among everyone). I encourage you to create a new standard operating procedure that "pay raises will never be given during employee reviews." Instead, give pay raises when they're warranted and keep the discussions during reviews to things that are going well, ways that individual can improve, and how the leadership team may be able to provide better support to the employee being reviewed. If you keep the issue of pay in performance reviews, just be aware that the people you're talking to may not be fully engaged in what you're saying because they're too occupied speculating how much they're going to get in their pay raise.

3. Please work with your executive team to make sure you're using techniques—other than money—to recognize or thank your employees for going above and beyond. Yes, the money is great and it needs to be there, but other forms of recognition are often times more appreciated by the recipient. If you've read White Paper 11, "The Great Huddle," then you already know about the importance of awards in your company.

4. Review your workers' compensation: If you haven't reviewed your workers' compensation

insurance in a while, it may be worth the investment of time in doing this. If you can reduce your workers' compensation insurance, you'll save money every single month—perhaps a significant amount of money! A good insurance agent can help guide you through this process, and it won't cost you a dime to research it.

5. Review your current health insurance benefits: As you know, the cost of health insurance has skyrocketed in recent years. If you haven't reviewed other options relative to health insurance plans within the past year, you really need to. Call in a couple different insurance salespeople, let them know what you're trying to accomplish (i.e., reduce costs), and ask them to give you their best suggestions on what you should do. Then, choose the idea you like the best and go with it!

SUMMARY

One of the first places to look to reduce costs is in your labor expenses. Labor costs are oftentimes the bulk of your corporate overhead. A slight reduction in your labor percentage can have a significant, favorable effect on your bottom-line profits.

Your people will make or break your business. You need to reward them for their efforts and treat them fairly. The point of the white paper is to make sure your compensation system is truly fair to everyone. Across-the-board pay raises aren't fair to your top producers. Giving pay raises simply because someone has worked at your company for another year is not necessarily fair to you. Allowing someone's pay to become out of line with her position sets her up for future pay cuts or termination; that's not fair to that person. It's important that you constantly recognize and reward people when goals are met or expectations are exceeded. But we have to remember that there are plenty of thoughtful, meaningful ways to thank people without simply throwing money at them, although the money does need to be there.

There are several other costs related to labor that may get out of line over time; we reviewed a couple of them. You very well may qualify for a different tier for your workers comp premiums; this could save your company a lot of money. Over the years, health insurance carriers have become creative in their product offerings to allow employers more flexibility and options in their health insurance coverage for their employees. It's absolutely worth looking into again if you haven't looked at it in the past year or two.

With the strategies and action steps presented in the white paper, you can set your company up for significant profitability increases. But please don't forget the biggest area of labor waste that was not mentioned in the white paper: employing people that simply aren't needed.

Everyone knows that, but when is the last time you took a hard look at everyone's roles and responsibilities and compared it to how much it's costing your company? Can you get the same job done with one less person?

If so, the entire cost of employing that person (salary, taxes, benefits, workers' comp insurance, etc.) can be saved and will flow directly to your bottom line—dollar for dollar!

Have you hired additional people to compensate for the weaknesses of others that should be doing that work, but for whatever reason can't or won't? If so, you're killing your profits. You have to make sure you get the right people in the right jobs. Otherwise, you'll be creating and recreating job descriptions based on your existing team members' talents and/or desires and this could be causing you to be overstaffed.

The white paper in this chapter was not intended to be the end-all for reducing labor costs. It was simply meant to get you thinking about some specific things and taking a couple deliberate actions to see how much you can reduce those costs. I strongly suggest you take more time to work on this with your leadership teams back at your businesses. Look every expense related to labor and question every one of them. It's highly likely you'll find money being wasted. I've literally seen companies double their annual net profits by paying closer attention to their labor expenses. It's that important!

Like everything, it's not easy and it will take time and focus. But you and your leadership team can do it and the rewards can be well worth the effort.

I wish you all the best as you go get unstuck!

STRATEGY 7

FINDING AND FILLING
THE PROFIT HOLES

Most companies do not have large single areas in their businesses where money (potential profits) pours out every month. I call those "large profit holes." Big problems are so alarming and have such an obvious impact on a company's survival that these types of problems are usually addressed and fixed quickly. That's great.

But on the flipside of this, most companies I've dealt with have *many* small profit holes that money trickles from every single month. Taken individually, none of these holes have a tremendous impact on the business. But collectively, they amount to a small fortune! In many companies, these little holes cost them more money than the companies earn in profits each year! That's important. Let me say it again: these little profit holes needlessly cost business owners more money than the business profits every single year! For every dollar these companies profit, at least a dollar is figuratively being thrown in the trash!

If you want to dramatically increase your profits, identifying and plugging the many little profit holes in your company will help you greatly. If your business is currently not profitable or worse, then this is a great place to begin to turn that around.

Wouldn't it be nice if you had only one place to look to find every single profit hole in your company? Well, I have great news for you: that place does exist! It is your company's income statement (profit and loss statement, also called your P&L). If you can pull up your company's P&L detail report, you'll see where every single penny comes in and goes out of your business. If you don't have the ability to do that, you need change that immediately by scheduling an appointment with your accountant. Having sound financial statements are critical to running any business.

The very top line of your income statement is "Income" (from sales). The bottom line is "Profit" or "Loss." Everything in between is where you'll find the profit holes! I'll give you an action step later that will return you to your own income statement, but for now, I'll outline some typical sections in your P&L where you just may find many profit holes. I'll also give you a series of questions for you to ask (and have answered) to determine which of these areas contain profit holes in your own company. Most importantly, though, these questions are provided to you as a guide to show you how to dig deep with your own questioning of each line on your income statement.

Let's start with the top of your income statement: "Income," which comes from sales.

Here are a few important questions that you should ask yourself: What would happen if you increased your pricing by just a little bit? Would you lose clients? Would a loss in clients necessarily hurt your profits, or would the price increase make a tremendous, favorable impact on your profitability?

Some people don't easily recognize how even a slight increase in pricing can have a significant impact on your profitability. Please consider this:

Pricing for Profitability

Scenario #1
In 2012, you sold widgets for $1.00 each. The total net cost to you (all overhead considered) was $.95

SALE PRICE:	$1.00
YOUR NET COST:	$.95
NET PROFIT:	$.05
NET PROFIT MARGIN:	5%

If annual sales were $1,000,000, then your net profit would be $50,000 (5%).

Scenario #2
In 2013, you decided to sell these same widgets for $1.03. The total net cost to you (all overhead considered) is still $.95

SALE PRICE:	$1.03
YOUR NET COST:	$.95
NET PROFIT:	$.08
NET PROFIT MARGIN:	8%

Assuming you lost no customers due to your price increase, then sales will be 3% higher in 2013 over 2012 (all other things remaining the same). That means, annual sales that were $1,000,000 automatically go up 3% to $1,030,000. Your 2013 profit margin went up to 8%, so your 2013 profit would be $82,400. An increase in net profit of $32,400!

Scenario #3

Let's presume that in 2013 you lost 20% of your customers due to your $.03 increase in pricing…

$1,000,000 x 80% = $800,000 x 1.03 (that adds your 3% price increase) = $824,000 in annual sales.

$824,000 x 8% net profit margin = an annual profit of $65,920.

So here's the question:

Would you rather earn $50,000 by producing $1,000,000 in work, or would you rather earn $65,920 on $824,000 in work?

I know the answer to the question is obvious. It's far better to do less work for more profit than to do more work for less profit. So what stops people from increasing their prices? In a word: fear.

As business owners, sometimes we actually negotiate against ourselves and set our pricing too low. Then we get stuck thinking that our customers will not be willing to pay us more, even as our own costs of doing business go up!

Listen, you may be right. Maybe your customers will ditch you for someone else if you raise your prices. But you owe it to yourself and to your company to at least have the courage to test that theory before you sell yourself on it.

Here's your first action step: Meet with your executive team and review all of the pricing you currently have in place. Again, by printing out the detail report of your P&L, you'll be able to see the unit price of everything.

Challenge yourself to find opportunities to increase pricing, even if it takes you a little bit outside of your comfort zone. From experience, I can tell you that more times than not, I've seen business owners make slight increases in their pricing and not lose a single customer because of it. Of course, I can't guarantee that for you, but I do encourage you to test the market from time to time instead of constantly negotiating the best deal you can for your customers.

To be clear, I'm not advocating taking advantage of your customers. But I am asking that you reconsider what it means to have a win-win relationship with your customers. Right now, you may have put yourself on the losing end of what should be a win/win relationship.

Now we'll go down to the lower portion of the income statement: "Expenses." Note: the following areas I'll cover may or may not be relevant to your business. The point of the questions that follow is to show you how to question each of the expense lines on your own company's income statement. The point is to "model" how to do it, so please don't worry if these examples aren't relevant to your own business.

Let's start with the line item that typically is the most expensive for a company: personnel costs (labor).

Personnel costs (or labor costs) are all of your costs associated with employing people. Here is a sampling of the questions you and your senior leaders may want to answer together relative to personnel costs:

- What are our total personnel costs (dollar volume)?

- How much do we invoice (sell) per employee (total sales revenue divided by the number of total full-time equivalent employees)?

- How can we increase that number?

- What is our labor ratio (total labor costs divided by total sales)?

- How can we reduce that number?

- How much overtime are we currently paying?

- Can we reduce overtime through smarter staffing and/or scheduling?

- Go through your employee roster and one by one, ask (and candidly answer), "Is this person earning too much for what they bring in the way of company benefit / profits," or "Are we overpaying this person?"

- Is our benefits package competitive, or is it too aggressive or too conservative based on comparable positions in our industry?

- What are the different health insurance options available to us?

- Who are our strongest players?

- Who are our weakest?

- What can we do about that?

- Could we produce the same quality and level of service for our customers if we had one less person on our payroll?

- Are our salespeople making us money or are they costing us money?

- Where else do we have "fat" in our labor and labor costs?

If applicable to your business, "Brokered Work" is another line on your income statement. *Brokered work* is a product or service that you sell, but don't produce in-house. Another way to state that is, it's the work that you resell. Here are the questions that need to be answered:

- How much are we marking up brokered work (what's our profit margin)?

- Can we increase that margin and still be competitive?

- When is the last time we researched new sources to produce the work we broker?

- Are we competitively bidding brokered work to different vendors?

- Are we brokering so much that we should consider bringing manufacturing of those products or services in-house?

- Are the orders we're brokering really worth the effort, or should we scale back, broker less, and focus more on our core products / services?

Equipment / Equipment Repair are the costs associated with the purchase, lease, and repairs of your production equipment (if applicable to your business). If you have production equipment, here are some questions that need to be answered:

- Do we have the right equipment for what we do, or are we using older, less productive equipment that is cheaper but is causing our production labor costs to be out of whack?

- Are our team members properly trained, and are they using the equipment in the most effective manner?

- Are there any features on our equipment that would help us a lot, but we don't use them because we don't know how?

- What are the costs vs. benefits (relative to labor costs) if we buy faster equipment?

- Have we bought state-of-the-art technology when we don't need all the bells and whistles? Could we buy a comparable piece of equipment without the features we don't need and, therefore, save money?

- Should we consider buying used equipment instead of new?

- Should we consider buying new equipment instead of used?

- Are there any pieces of equipment that we're holding onto that are now obsolete for what we do? Can we sell it or trade it in?

- Do we consistently bid our equipment purchases to multiple vendors, or have we limited ourselves by being overly loyal to just one vendor?

- Would service agreements save us money in the long run?

- Are service agreements costing us more than if we just paid for each repair as it became necessary?

- Are we paying excessively for after-hours service contracts when we don't really need them?

- Should we be taking advantage of after-hour service rather than having the equipment down and losing production time?

- Should we train one of our own employees to be able to service our equipment?

- Are there areas in our business that we could automate with new equipment that would provide a return on investment greater than doing these jobs manually?

- Would we be better off outsourcing functions rather than paying huge fixed costs for equipment that's rarely used?

Production Supplies are the supplies needed to produce your products. If you purchase and use production supplies, then please ask yourself the following:

- Are we competitively bidding these purchases or just sending blanket purchase orders over to vendors we've used for a long time?

- Where do we have excessive production supply waste?

- Do we lose supplies due to damage?

- Are we keeping good inventory on hand, or are we running out at the last minute or paying rush-service fees to get supplies delivered same day? How much production time are we losing due to poor supply inventory management?

- Are we tying up cash and valuable work space by ordering too many supplies at a time?

- Are we taking advantage of volume purchases and fast-pay discounts?

- Are we buying inferior supplies in an effort to save money but end up costing us more money due to projects having to be rerun or returned by our customers?

- Can we find less expensive products that would accomplish the same thing as our existing, higher-end supplies?

- Do we have too many people making the purchases to the point where we've lost control over purchasing?

- Are we still using vendors that consistently deliver late and send us wrong orders?

- Are we considering the necessity of specialty supplies when quoting customer projects?

- Do we have proper supply inventory tracking, or is there a chance some of our stuff is "walking out of here"?

- Can we buy our supplies from online sources, such as e-bay?

Sales and Marketing Expenses are the costs associated with selling or marketing your products or services; including advertising. Please ask yourself the following questions:

- After analyzing our advertising costs, are we certain we're getting an appropriate return on our investment?

- Do we track the results of our advertising?

- Is our advertising message fresh and relevant, or are we simply using old artwork over and over?

- Are we negotiating to reduce our marketing and advertising expenses or simply paying sticker price?

- Are our salespeople getting great results and earning us money, or are we throwing money away on paying salespeople that aren't getting results?

- Do we have an effective sales and marketing plan?

- Are we marketing to the right demographic, or are we simply sprinkling marketing money around in the same places we always have?

- Do we belong to associations that we don't even attend or that don't get us results?

- Are we providing our salespeople the correct sales training they need in order to get better results?

- Should we hire another sales rep?

- Should we consider using an independent rep?

- How do our sales and marketing efforts compare to our best competitor's?

Automobile expenses are the costs associated with either company owned vehicles or personal vehicles that are used for company business and require reimbursement to the owner. If you have company vehicles or if you reimburse your employees for using their own vehicles, then please ask yourself the following questions:

- When is the last time we looked into other vehicle options for our company vehicles? Are we simply buying the same vehicles we've always bought, or are we making sure we're not over- or underbuying?

- Do we consider fuel efficiency when choosing our vehicles?

- Are we properly maintaining our fleet? Should we consider outsourcing fleet maintenance?

- Do we provide our drivers GPS or are they still printing out from Mapquest or using a map (causing wasted time)?

- Are we properly controlling the use of our company gas card?

- Are we paying employees mileage reimbursement when it would be less expensive to just buy another company vehicle?

- Are we paying for company vehicles when it would be less expensive to pay reimbursement to our employees for using their own vehicles?

- Do we have the proper amount of insurance on our vehicles? Is our deductible where it should be?

- Do we understand the potential liabilities from the use of personal vehicles?

- Have we invested in driver safety training to protect our drivers and reduce our insurance costs?

- Are all of our company vehicles safe (including good tires)?

- Are we taking advantage of our company vehicles for marketing benefits (decals, vehicle-wraps, signs, etc.)?

- Are our company vehicles kept clean inside and out?

- Do we perform preventive maintenance, or do we just wait until something breaks?

- Have we made sure all our drivers have a valid driver's license?

- Are our company vehicles being used for personal reasons by our employees?

- Do we have written policies regarding the use of company vehicles?

- Do we drug and alcohol test our drivers?

- Are we following all local, state, and federal laws regarding our vehicles?

- Should we look into GPS vehicle tracking to have better accountability of our vehicles' whereabouts throughout the day or night?

Okay, those are several questions from just six lines that you may find on your own income statement. There are literally scores of other lines that will require you to review in detail as we've done here.

Here's your action step: Schedule a meeting with your executive team with the objective of identifying and filling the many little profit holes that money pours from each month at your company. I suggest you set a revenue savings goal as well. For example, if your total annual expenses (from last year's income statement) are $3,000,000, then you could set a goal of reducing expenses by 3.5%. 3.5% of $3,000,000 equals $105,000! That's not just $105,000 in reduced expenses; remember that every single dollar in reduced expenses (all other things remaining the same) equals a dollar for dollar increase in your net profit! And those savings carry over from year to year, further compounding the return on your investment of time.

Just think how much of your product or service you would have to deliver to increase your profits so significantly!

If the six areas of your income statement that we addressed today are not relevant to your particular company, just look at your own income statement and do the same thing we did here. Ask as many thoughtful questions as you can about each purchase indicated on your income statement to make sure you're being as smart as you can be with your money.

The next time your executive team convenes, go line by line through your own income statement and ask as many thoughtful questions as you can about each line as I did in the examples provided.

As you answer those questions, action steps will be developed and assigned to the different members of your executive team. As you know, results don't come from great planning alone; they come from executing your plans, measuring the results, and adjusting your plans when necessary.

This will take a considerable amount of time, effort, focus, and discipline, but you can do it. And the outcome could be a significant increase in your annual profits and in your company value.

I wish you all my best!

REVIEW / ACTION STEPS

1. Consider raising your prices: Meet with your executive team to reconsider your current pricing. Is there a chance you may be leaving money on the table? When is the last time you raised your pricing? What are your competitor's charging? If you determine that you should raise some of your pricing or all of your pricing, go ahead and do it! And remember, every penny of that increase will directly impact your net profit margin significantly. Even slight price increases can have a significantly favorable impact on your net profits and profit margin.

2. Meet with your executive team and set a cost-reduction goal. Then, analyze and question every single line on your company P&L to see where you may be able to make smarter purchasing decisions and therefore, increase profitability through reducing costs or increasing efficiencies. This will take a significant amount of time. Please don't rush it! Take your time, be creative, and be open to doing things differently than you have in the past. Remember, if you want different results, you have to change your thinking and your processes. This is well worth the effort! Please be sure to quantify your expected cost reductions or benefits of increased efficiencies so you can determine where you stand relative to the goal you set for yourself.

SUMMARY

Everyone knows the value of money and of positive cash flow. But as business owners, we sometimes tend to negotiate against ourselves when it comes to pricing. Likewise, we occasionally neglect to reconsider all the areas where we spend our money. We assume that we're doing the right things with our money, but without a periodic self-audit, it's only a matter of time until your company has many small profit holes that cost you a fortune each year.

By using your executive team to assist you in identifying and then planning, executing, measuring, and adjusting your pricing and cost-reduction measures, a couple things happen. First, you'll increase your profits by increasing your sales margin and by reducing costs. The second thing that happens is that your executive team members will become more profit-conscious. This initiative will really open everyone's eyes to how modest adjustments can have such a significant impact on your company's profits and profit margin.

You and your team work too hard for your money to allow any of it to be squandered away. By taking action now, you can immediately begin to grow your bottom line.

Go get unstuck! I wish you my best!

STRATEGY 8

IMPROVING OUTSIDE SALES

This white paper is intended for business owners that currently have outside salespeople, but are frustrated with the poor results those salespeople have been getting.

The salespeople always seem busy, but their results are disappointing. Whenever you confront them on their lack of new sales, they do a wonderful job of "selling you" on the fact that they have some great stuff on the fence that's about to land! So you wait. And you wait some more while they stay busy looking like they're really busy. A few months go by, and then you confront them again. What do they say? The same exact thing they did last time and the cycle continues. And you wait again. Sound familiar?

Maybe you've been a salesperson before, but that was a long time ago. Or you've never been a salesperson yourself and you aren't confident in your ability to manage salespeople. You think you have a great salesperson, but something just doesn't feel right. *How can this salesperson appear to work so hard but have such poor results?* Let's explore that question!

Being a salesperson is a very hard job, especially when it's done right.

Think about it: Salespeople don't have the luxury of coming in to a structured day of work unless they structure it themselves. Salespeople don't have work waiting for them; they have to create the work themselves! Salespeople are faced with rejection on a daily basis. Have you ever noticed that great salespeople like to work with other people? Well, the truth is, salespeople spend an enormous amount of time alone!

To be great at sales, you have to be incredibly disciplined. There is nobody following you around all day to make sure you're doing what you should be doing. You have to be organized, passionate, smart, well-spoken, mentally tough, and you must be committed to growing revenue. But even all that is not enough to be great at sales.

First off, you have to have a sales system. Think of all the other areas of your business that have systems. Now imagine if none of those systems existed. People were just told to start producing. How effective would they be? The obvious answer is that they wouldn't be nearly as effective. Systems are critical in every area of your business, including sales. Unfortunately, having a sales system is often overlooked in small businesses.

What is a sales system? *It is an outline of the all the necessary steps that need to be taken in order to move someone from being a prospect to becoming a customer.* Each one of these steps has a purpose and a specific objective (goal).

For example, the first step in your sales system could be the cold call. The purpose of the cold call may be to find out if the prospect company has a need for your product or service. This is called qualifying the prospect. If the prospect doesn't have a need for what you're selling, then your salesperson needs to know that right away so no additional time is wasted in trying to sell to someone that will never buy from you.

If on the cold call, your salesperson finds out that, indeed, they do have a need for your product or service (and are likely already getting it from a competitor of yours), then the purpose of the call is to find out the name and title of the person at the prospect-company that makes the final decision in purchasing your specific product or service. The objective, then, of the cold call is to (1) qualify the prospect company, and (2) if qualified as a prospect (potential buyer), find out the name and title of the decision maker.

Okay, great. Now what? Well, the second step in the sales system could be the warm call. This is when your salesperson makes initial contact with the decision maker. The purpose of this call could be to (1) requalify and make sure the person you're talking to truly is the final decision maker. Once you qualify that the company does have a need for your product or service and you really are talking to the final decision maker, your next objective of the warm call could be (2) to gather important information from the decision maker such as how much of your competitors products or services they're currently buying (how big a prospect are they), and (3) to ask some smart, probing questions in order to determine some areas of "pain" the prospect may have with their current vendor, (4) give the prospect a powerful benefit you may be able to provide him/her, and (5) to get permission from the decision maker allowing you to get some information to that person and call back in a week or so with another phone call. The objective of this step, then, is to "get permission to take info and call back."

The next step in your sales system could be the hot call. Objective (goal) of hot call: to schedule a face-to-face appointment with the decision maker.

The next step after that might be the appointment. The objective of the appointment may be to get a signed contract. Or it may be to get a commitment from the prospect to give you a try the next time they need your product / service. Or it may be to schedule another appointment to give a full-blown product presentation and a formal proposal.

The particular steps in your sales system are dependent on your industry or your individual company and need to be tailored as such. No matter, it is imperative your salespeople have a system to follow. Note: a sample sales system is provided in the action steps at the end of this white paper. Feel free to use this sample as guide in developing your own sales system.

So the first step in answering the question, "How can my salesperson appear to work so hard but have such poor results?" is to make sure a system exists and that your salespeople are trained and know how to execute the system. If and when they have a sales system, you're off to a good start! But that alone is not enough!

Once the system is in place and your sales team is trained in it, they need a "point system" that will keep them focused on doing the most important things with their precious time. When you use a point system, your salespeople can taste small victories along the way to the final victory: making a sale.

Remember, the ultimate goal is to "make sales" and "increase revenue," thereby, increasing profits. But there's something called a "sales cycle" that needs to be considered. The sales cycle is *the average amount of time it takes to move someone from being a prospect to becoming a paying customer.*

If you're selling office supplies, for example, the sales cycle may be very short. Since many of your prospects order office supplies every week, you have an opportunity every week to get them as a customer.

But other industries have much longer sales cycles. For example, if you sell jet engines to aircraft manufacturers, they may contract to buy this product only once every three years. If that's the case, then you'll have to wait up to three years just to have a chance to make a sale, even after they've committed that they're interested in buying from you!

Obviously, you can't just sit around for years waiting for a deal. You have to continue to hunt to find other opportunities. Even if you sell office supplies, you can't wait around hoping that the prospect will buy from you next week. No matter how long or how short your sales cycle is, salespeople have to constantly fill the sales funnel. In other words, salespeople need to keep finding prospects and continually move those prospect-accounts through the sales system you've created. Sometimes, that's difficult to do unless you have an accountability tool to guide behavior.

In case you haven't noticed, most salespeople tend to be competitive. They like results and they like them quickly. Without tangible results (i.e., new customers) from their activity, they can become frustrated.

To keep them motivated and focused on important sales activities, create a point system for them. The point system is where you award points based on executing the specific steps in your sales system. The more time-consuming steps earn higher points. Easier steps, such as making a cold call, earn fewer points.

Of course, the most points should be awarded for the ultimate victory: Earning a new customer!

As an example point system, using the hypothetical sales system outlined above, your point system may look like this:

- Cold Call: 1 point (if objective is met)
- Warm Call: 2 points (if objective is met)
- Hot Call: 5 points (if objective is met)
- Attending an appointment: 10 points
- Scheduling a follow-up presentation: 5 points
- Making a follow-up presentation: 10 points
- Follow-up phone calls: 1 point
- Earning a new customer: 20 points

Then, pick a number of points you think are the minimum allowable points in a day. For example, you may determine that your salesperson must earn a minimum of 40 points per day (averaged each week).

Also, be sure to pick a number of points that constitute an "exceptionally great" day! The best salespeople are more motivated to have an "exceptional day" rather than to simply "exceed the minimum." It's psychological, I know. But that's how salespeople think; trust me!

Let's recap what we've done so far: First, we asked the question, "How can my salesperson appear to work so hard but have such poor results?" The first answer to that question is that your salesperson may not have a sales system. We discussed how to create a sales system. Next, we addressed the necessity of having a point system in place so your salespeople can have activity goals and know where they stand relative to those goals. A point system not only motivates salespeople, it also keeps them focused on doing the right things with their time. Now, we'll address a third common mistake many businesses owners make: they don't equip their salespeople with proper contact management systems.

Simply put, a contact management system is a tool for salespeople to use to help them manage their contacts (prospects) efficiently. In the olden days, salespeople used paper systems including index cards, post-it notes, notes on the back of business cards, scrap pieces of paper, and the like.

Today, there are many powerful computer-based contact management systems on the market (also referred to as contact database management systems or contact records management systems, CRMs.). If your salespeople don't have this tool, they're getting eaten up by your competitors' salespeople that do use an electronic system!

A contact database management system is computer software that acts as an electronic rolodex, but with many powerful features. For example, each prospect is assigned an ID Status by your salespeople. By providing an ID Status for each prospect in the system, your salespeople can look up contacts according to where they stand in the sales cycle. For example, if your salesperson wants to make cold calls, he can find the group of people he's looking to cold call simply by clicking the lookup button and then entering Cold Call. All of the prospects that need to be cold called that are in the database will pop up. Each step in your sales system is mirrored in the ID Status lookup feature of your software. This keeps your salespeople organized, giving them a huge competitive advantage.

Furthermore, this software provides a notes tab, which allows your salespeople to see all of the notes that were entered after every interaction with each prospect. Nothing is left to memory. These notes are critical for salespeople in deciding what tactic to employ next to move the prospect to becoming a customer.

There are alarm settings for prospects in the database that will pop up at the date/time your salesperson sets. For example, if the prospect asked your salesperson to call back in two weeks, the salesperson sets an alarm that will remind the salesperson to call the prospect two weeks later. Salespeople spend their valuable time moving people through the sales system; a contact database management system prevents prospects from falling through the cracks, thereby wasting all the time that was invested into the prospect up to that point.

In addition to helping your salespeople organize contacts, this software also allows your salespeople or sales managers to instantly pull up reports, which are valuable in tracking activity. With networked versions of the software or Web-based versions, sales managers can pull up and monitor activities even if their sales team operates in different states or even different countries! Furthermore, your salespeople can work with the same database when in the office, at their homes, or while travelling.

Some popular contact database management systems include Act, GoldMine, and Salesforce, just to name a few. If your salespeople currently don't have a tool like this, please make it a point to explore the different options available to you. It's well worth the modest investment!

We've addressed three major reasons salespeople seem to work so hard, but have poor results: (1) lack of a sales system, (2) lack of an activity point system, and (3) lack of a contact database management system. Those are big ones, but here's a short list of other things to consider when diagnosing your salespeople's specific challenges along with some proposed solutions to consider:

Problem (4): Salespeople that don't have solid selling-skills. Solution: Enroll them into a sales training program. This requires an investment of time and money, but if you think your salespeople are otherwise committed to your company, this may be a wise investment for you to make.

Problem (5): Salespeople don't have adequate product knowledge or company knowledge. Solution: Teach them! Make sure they know your product inside and out! They should also be familiar with your competitors' products or services. There's nothing more frustrating than talking with a salesperson that has little industry and/or product knowledge. Your salespeople should also know your company's history, market position, and the competitive differentiators that will allow that person to passionately sell his/her prospects on why that person should want to do business with your company. Have your salespeople spend some time working in different departments in your company. Have them work in production, customer service, shipping, and any other departments that directly touch your customers. With this additional, firsthand knowledge, your salespeople will be much better equipped to bring in new customers.

Problem (6): Your salespeople don't have an adequate "hit list" of prospects to call on. If your salespeople have small or old lists of prospects to call on, those lists become stale and difficult to be effective with. Please be sure your salespeople are continually adding new prospects in their CRM system. When they have a large list of prospects to call on, your salespeople will be much more effective.

Problem (7): Your salespeople are simply not ever going to be great salespeople. Solution: Replace them immediately. This problem is more common than people would like to admit. It's also the most costly. Listen, some people simply aren't cut out to be outside sales representatives. No matter how great your sales system, no matter how many tools and how much training you provide them, they'll never be great. They don't have the inherent skills necessary to be great at sales. At the beginning of this white paper, you read about a few of those characteristics: "Disciplined, organized, passionate, smart, well-spoken, mentally tough, and committed to growing revenue." If any one of those characteristics is missing, a person could be doomed to mediocrity at best as an outside sales representative. If two or more of those personality traits are absent, you'd probably being doing everyone a favor by encouraging that person to find a new profession where he or she can excel.

This white paper does not cover every single possible reason salespeople seem to work so hard, but have poor results. We've touched on some big ones, but there certainly are other potential reasons. If you're still not sure what to do next, I suggest you have a private conversation with your ineffective salesperson (salespeople) and ask them straight out, "Why aren't you having better results?" Don't accept that "things are on the fence and about to land." Instead, keep the conversation focused on why it's taking them so long to close new business. The answers you get from this conversation should assist you in deciding what to do next. Just make darn sure your salesperson and you leave this meeting with an agreed upon and tangible next step. If your salespeople aren't bringing in new business in a timely manner, something's broken. You have to take specific action to fix it because it won't go away by itself. That's a fact.

It will take time and possibly even emotion. It won't be easy. But you can do it!

REVIEW / ACTION STEPS

1. Please make sure your salespeople have a written sales system or sales model to follow. Here is a sample sales system to help you in creating your own:

   XYZ Company - Sales System

   I. Cold Call: the objective of the cold call is to (1) qualify the prospect company (do they buy what you sell?), and (2) if qualified as a potential buyer, find out the name and title of the decision maker.

   II. Warm Call: the objective of the warm call is to (1) requalify and make sure the person you're talking to truly is the final decision maker, (2) gather important information from the decision maker such as how much of your competitors' products or services they're currently buying (are they a big prospect or a little one?), (3) ask probing questions to get the decision maker to tell you the areas of "pain" they have with their current vendor, (4) get permission from the decision maker to get him/her some information and to follow up next week with another phone call.

III. Information Drop: the objective is simply to get information to the decision maker.

IV. Hot Call: the objective of the hot call is to schedule a face-to-face appointment with the decision maker at a specific date and time.

V. The Appointment: The objective of the appointment is to get a signed contract (or to get a commitment to purchase from you the next time they buy or to schedule another appointment to make a full-blown presentation, whichever of these objectives best meets your requirements).

VI. Follow-Up Call: The objective of the follow-up call is to (1) reconnect with the decision maker so he/she does not forget about you, (2) to get a recommitment from the decision maker to buy from you next time he/she purchases your goods or services, and (3) to get permission to follow-up again on a certain date if you haven't heard from the decision maker first.

2. Create a point system to keep your salespeople focused on doing the right things to generate revenue. A point system is also an effective accountability tool that sales managers and/or business owners should use. Here is a sample

point system that you can use to get ideas in creating your own:

-Sample Point System-

- Cold Call: 1 point (if objective is met)
- Warm Call: 2 points (if objective is met)
- Info-Drop: 4 points (if objective is met)
- Hot Call: 5 points (if objective is met)
- Attending an appointment: 10 points
- Scheduling a follow-up presentation: 5 points
- Making a follow-up presentation: 10 points
- Follow-up phone calls: 1 point
- Earning a new customer: 20 points
- Minimum acceptable daily points = 40 points per day (averaged each week)
- Outstanding results = 47+ points per day (averaged each week)

3. If your salespeople do not currently have a computer-based contact database management system, then please look into buying one. The benefits of having this are significant and the cost in purchasing this software is typically between $150 and $2,000, depending on whether you want stand-alone systems or networked versions (including "the cloud") and depending on how much other functionality you want or need. My

suggestion is to start simple and move up later if/when you want to.

4. Make sure your salespeople have the sales training they need in order to be most effective. If you can handle this yourself, great. But if you don't have vast experience in outside sales or in sales management, then you should seriously consider outsourcing this training.

5. Be sure your salespeople have enough product knowledge to be able to differentiate your product or service from that of your competitors. That means they need to know your products or services inside and out, and they also need to know your competitors' products or services just as well.

6. Please make sure your salespeople know about your company history and your overall operating system. If your salespeople don't know your company history and aren't able to sell people as to why your company is the best to work with (i.e., your quality control processes), they're at a distinctive disadvantage to your competitors who do know their companies' strengths.

7. Please be sure your salespeople have a large database of prospects to call on. If their lists are too small, it is highly likely they'll spend more time on disqualified non-prospects because they don't know who else to call on. Make sure they have a large prospect-base and also be sure

they continually update it as new prospects are identified.

8. If you've done everything you can to set your salespeople up for success and one or more of them still isn't producing results, you have to let them go. There's nothing more costly than carrying salespeople that don't produce. It wastes your money and demoralizes and angers your other team members. Please remember, good intentions are nice, but results are required.

SUMMARY

If you have poorly performing or even just mediocre performing outside sales representatives, you really need to address it.

This white paper addressed some common reasons salespeople suffer and the tools that can help them improve. Listen, if you want better sales results, but aren't providing the right tools, you're setting your salespeople up to fail. Please don't do that!

It is just too expensive to have ineffective salespeople. Frankly, the other departments in your company will begin to resent the sales team if the results aren't there. You're not the only one that notices poor sales performance and you're not the only one that's frustrated by it.

Outside sales is a very tough job, both mentally and emotionally. It's demoralizing to have doors slammed in your face day after day. So please do all you can to make sure your salespeople have all the tools they need to have doors open for them instead. You win, they win, and your entire team wins! It's well worth the effort.

If you have a salesperson that's still not cutting it even after you've provided them all the necessary tools and training, then you have a responsibility to move that person to a job more suited for him or her, either inside or outside of your company.

Sales cycles can be long or short, depending on your particular industry. New salespeople absolutely need time to fill their funnel of prospects and it takes time to build relationships. Once your new salespeople are trained and equipped to do the job, you have to be patient as they go shake things up. Be patient and encouraging. And when the new orders start coming in, be sure to make a big deal out of it! Your salespeople will appreciate you celebrating with them when they bring in new accounts.

While it's important to be patient with new salespeople, you also have to listen to your gut. If you believe that your salespeople appear to be busy but aren't getting the results you expect, then you have to address it professionally. This white paper showed you how to do that.

This isn't easy to do. It does require time, effort, and even some money. But if you're going to do it, do it right. I wish you all my best as you go get your sales unstuck.

STRATEGY 9

RALLYING YOUR TEAM AROUND A GOAL

If you were to ask each person that works at your company, "What is our company goal?" how many different answers do you think you'd get?

If the answer is "more than one," or, "we don't have a company goal," then you have a big opportunity in front of you!

Whenever a team of people is expected to work together in synchronicity and to give their best individual efforts toward success, then success needs to be clearly defined. Otherwise, each individual is forced to rely on his or her individual perception of what defines success.

Think about that for a minute. If I were to ask you to define what success means to each of your individual team members, could you do it? Not without guessing you couldn't, unless, of course, they specifically told you how they define it.

The same is true with your employees. They can't possibly know how *you* define success unless *you* clearly define it for them. By setting a specific goal, everyone is on the same page relative to what constitutes success.

A goal is much more powerful than a hope, and there are certain requirements in order for you to have a true goal. We'll cover those now.

First of all, a goal must be *valuable*. That's obvious. It also has to be *attainable*. If your objective is so far out of reach that it's impossible, it's not a goal, it's just hype.

A goal also has to be *measurable*. In other words, you can't use platitudes. For example, to say, "Our goal is to be the best" is not a goal because it's not measurable. How do you define what the best is? How do you know if you've achieved it? Without measurements, you can't! To take that example a little further, if you say you have a goal to "be very profitable," you don't have a goal. The word *very* has different meanings to different people.

In order for your goal to be measurable, it needs to be specific and have objective metrics attached. Instead of saying, "Our goal is to be very profitable," you would attach measurements and instead say, "Our goal is to profit $200,000." When you do that, everyone's clear; if you profited $199,000, you did not succeed in your goal. If you profited $200,000, you did.

So a goal needs to be valuable, attainable, and measureable. It also must be *committed to memory* by everyone that's striving to reach the goal. If people can't remember what the goal is, they certainly aren't driven by it! If they aren't driven by it, then why bother even having a goal?

The next ingredient for having a goal is that you must attach a *date* to it. In order for a goal to be real, there must be an end date. Otherwise, there's no sense of urgency to motivate people. If you say your goal is to "profit $200,000" that probably feels good, but it does little to inspire your troops. After all, they have forever to get that done! If you say that your goal is to "profit $200,000 this year," then everyone's clear; it you don't do it this year, you didn't reach your goal. Likewise, if you do achieve it this year, you won!

Okay, let's recap: In order for you to have a goal, it must be valuable, attainable, measureable, committed to memory by everyone that's going after the goal, and you must have an end date or date of attainment. Now there's just one more ingredient in order for you to have a true goal. Here it is: Every single person going after the goal must have a *burning desire* to achieve it. Let that sink in for a minute. I didn't say that everyone hopes to hit the goal or that people really want to hit the goal; I said, "People have to have a *burning desire* to achieve it."

So there they are; all of the ingredients necessary to have a true goal: It must be (1) valuable, (2) attainable, (3) measureable, (4) committed to memory by everyone that's going after the goal, (5) it must have an end date to determine whether or not the goal was achieved and (6) everyone must have a burning desire to achieve the goal.

If any of your existing goals do not contain all of these elements, then you really don't have a goal, you have a hope. There is little power behind hope as compared to the power you can derive from a true goal.

So here's your first action step: If you already have what you thought was a company goal, but it doesn't contain all the elements of a true goal, then you need to adjust it so that it does. If you're hung up on the burning desire element of a goal, I understand. How are you supposed to instill a burning desire in all of your people, even if you already have it yourself? I get it. Please stay with me; we'll get there. If you're a person that currently doesn't have any specified goals, then you absolutely need to create one.

Human nature is not driven by whatever the wind may bring. We're instinctively programmed with a certain degree of competitiveness in our spirits. That's a wonderful thing and you need to tap into that power. As a great leader, you have to facilitate the creation of goals with your team. Your people need goals in order to give their best. They need to give their best in order for them to rise above mediocrity and have passion in their work.

This isn't hype, folks; this is real and it's very important.

If you're the type of person that thinks that goal setting is a bunch of hype, let me tell you unequivocally: true goals work.

If you've set goals in the past and they haven't worked out for you, the first thing I want you to do is to honestly ask yourself if your goals were valuable, attainable, measureable, committed to memory with a date of achievement and a burning desire to achieve them? If they fit all those criteria and you still fell short, I want you to ask yourself a couple more questions:

Where do you think you would have ended up if you hadn't had the advantage of being driven by that goal? Do you think your results would have been as good as they were? In the end of it all, was your goal really a waste of time, or did you benefit from it even while not necessarily achieving it?

I think if you're honest in your answers, you now see the power in having true goals. The art of setting a true goal will never guarantee victory. But what it does guarantee is that you'll be much better off in the end with a true goal than if you never set a goal at all. Furthermore, when you're team goes after a goal together, the bonding and ingenuity that takes place is far better than if you never had a goal to begin with, even if you don't actually hit your objective.

There's an old saying: "If you don't know where you're going, any road will get you there." That's exactly right. And if your people are all taking their own roads, then you cannot possibly have synchronicity. You have fragmentation, which will lead to conflicts, which will lead to drama, turnover, wasted time, money, and opportunity, and all the other garbage that business owners resent.

Before I continue, I hope you don't mind if I just keep things honest with a reality check. If your business has conflict, drama, turnover, wasted time, money, and opportunity, then you have nobody to blame but yourself, and I guarantee you don't have a true goal that everyone is rallied around; a goal that's valuable, attainable, measurable, committed to memory by everyone, a date of achievement, and everyone having a burning desire to achieve it. If that's you, please stay with me because you can fix it.

The most challenging thing to do is to rally a group of different people around the same goal. What's valuable to one person may not be valuable enough to another to have a burning desire to achieve it. So how do you, as the top leader in your company, get your entire team rallied around a single, meaningful, true goal?

You must do these eight things:

1. Involve the team in the process.

2. Make sure they know what's in it for them (rewards).

3. Once everyone buys into the goal, make it the standard; if people don't own it, they don't belong on your team.

4. Lead by example with your own commitment and enthusiasm.

5. Invest time teaching people how to win.

6. Keep a scoreboard and talk about it all the time.

7. Set stepping-stone goals (guideposts) along the way and celebrate each win as they happen.

8. Keep your word and pay up!

Let's briefly cover each of those eight strategies in getting everyone on your team rallied around the same goal.

The first requirement is to *involve the team in the process*. That means, get them involved in deciding on the actual true goal. Don't just dictate a goal to them. This will require you to be candid with everyone regarding the state of your company. By sharing the realities in your company with your team, you can lead them, rather than dictate to them, in creating a goal that is truly meaningful to you, your company, and to your team.

As you're working with your team to nail down a goal that is meaningful to everyone, you need to *make sure that each of your team members knows what's in it for them to achieve it.* I'm talking about rewards! If in reaching your goal, you personally win and your company as a whole wins, that's great. But if you don't allow each person on your team to personally win as well, then the burning desire to achieve it just won't be where it needs to be. That's fair. So tie meaningful rewards to achieving the goal so that everyone has skin in the game. In doing this, you'll not only motivate people to give their personal best efforts in achieving the goal, you'll simultaneously create a culture where team members will hold each other accountable to giving their best too. After all, they know what's in it for them and they're not going to idly sit by and watch other people blow it for them!

Once you and your team create your company goal, and once everyone knows what's in it for them to win, *you have to make sure everyone "owns" the goal.* Let them know right from the start that your intention is for the team to win and for everyone to earn the rewards. Let them know that you are deeply committed to this and you expect the same from them. Make sure everyone knows that you plan to cater to the people that are equally as committed to it as you are. Then follow through. If and when anyone on your team seems to have lost the passion for the goal or has slipped back into their old ways, you have to immediately address it with them. Do everything you can to coach them back into line. If you find yourself continually frustrated by the same person that doesn't seem to be engaged in reaching your goal, then you have a responsibility to protect the other team members from this person's lack of commitment. Remember, if you can't change your people, change your people with other people who share your vision.

Now let's talk about you. You're the leader or the head of the organization. If you want your team to honestly and vigorously go after a goal together, then *you have to lead by example with your own self-commitment and enthusiasm.* If your team thinks you've abandoned the goal, they'll abandon it too. You can never expect anyone on your team to do something that you aren't willing to do yourself. Even though you're the boss, you lose all moral authority if you don't lead by example. The best leaders already know this, though, so I'm probably just preaching to the choir! Just make sure you show your excitement in doing the things necessary to reach your goal. Talk about the goal frequently and passionately and give your personal best efforts every single day.

Personal commitment and burning desire are necessary when going after a true goal. But beyond that, *you also have to make sure that your team knows how to win!* It's your job to make sure that happens. For example, if your company's true goal is to "Increase net profits by 7 percent this calendar year over last calendar year," then you have to make sure everyone knows how to increase net profits. You may think it's obvious to everyone, and you can even be sure that everyone knows some of the ways to increase net profits, but there will be few people on your team that know all the ways to increase net profits at your company. You need to teach them.

Have staff meetings where the agenda is to identify all of the ways your team can increase net profits. Talk about individual accountability and discipline, efficiencies, reducing waste, increasing pricing, not having to rerun projects or give them away for free. Talk about smarter purchasing and better negotiating. Talk about how much money it costs your company when a fifteen-minute break turns into twenty minutes or a half-hour lunch turns into forty minutes!

Talk about proper maintenance of your equipment. Talk about taking care of supplies and keeping an organized workplace. Talk about everything you and your team can think of to increase profits by 7 percent by the end of the year so that everyone can enjoy the rewards that come with that! I'm not talking about a single staff meeting. I'm talking about allocating a portion of every staff meeting to brainstorming, discussing, and teaching ways to win the game. I can't stress the importance of this enough. You have to make sure your people know how to win; otherwise, their good intentions just won't be enough to get you to where you all want to be.

Okay, you involved your team in the process of setting the goal. You attached rewards to reaching the goal and everyone has skin in the game. You've committed yourself to holding everyone accountable for their best efforts and you're leading by example with your own commitment and enthusiasm. On top of that, you're providing ongoing training to teach your team how to accomplish the goal. Now, *you need a scoreboard!*

Everyone on your team needs to know where the team stands relative to the goal at all times. Using the example goal of "increasing net profits by 7 percent this calendar year over last year," the scoreboard could be a posting of monthly net profits vs. same time period last year, as well as year-to-date net profits vs. last year-to-date net profits. By doing this, people (including you) will know whether you're on track to achieve the goal or whether you need to make additional adjustments to get on track.

In addition to the scoreboard, you should also brainstorm with your team the reasons you're either on track or off track. Talk about the specific improvements your team has made that has favorably affected the scoreboard. Conversely, have candid discussions with them about the things that are holding your team back from being on track. This goes back to teaching your team how to win.

Keeping a scoreboard is critical for you and your team to have more control over reaching your goal. Without one, you're all hoping you win in the end, but as you know, there's little power behind a hope, so keep score!

A great way to keep people engaged in reaching the goal is to provide the opportunity for small wins and celebrations along the way. *You should set stepping-stone goals or guidepost goals and reward your team when they hit them.* Your guidepost goals, using the above example goal of increasing net profits by 7 percent this calendar year over last year, could be to give quarterly rewards if the quarter is 7 percent more profitable than the same time period last year. Or you could set guidepost goals that focus more on activity rather than just the result.

For example, if your team determined that they have an opportunity to reduce labor costs in pursuit of increasing net profits by 7 percent, then you could use your company's labor ratio (total labor costs divided by total sales revenue) as a guidepost goal. If they can reduce the labor ratio by X percent each fiscal quarter over last year, then they win the guidepost goal and they get rewarded. The biggest rewards come when the actual goal is met, but smaller rewards are provided when the guidepost goals are hit. I know this is obvious to you, but I'll say it anyway: if people can taste victory along the way, they'll stay involved because they want to taste it even more. Please make sure you provide them those opportunities.

Finally, we come to the end. In the example goal we've discussed, it's the end of the year and the results are in: You won! Now it's time to pay up! I'm not talking about burying the reward inside everyone's paycheck; I'm talking about a dramatic presentation of bonus checks in a celebratory environment. As you're making the reward presentations, use it as an opportunity to teach people some more. Talk about what each person did, specifically, to help your team win. Talk about the things the company did together that made this celebration and the rewards come to fruition. You've probably seen a final World Series game in baseball or a Super Bowl in football. What happens when the team wins? They celebrate! Champagne is flowing, and in the interviews, you'll hear the players and the coaches' talk about how they won. They talk about what they did well, but they also talk about what they need to improve on in the off-season! What you may not know is that each player and coach on the winning team is also the recipient of a large bonus check! It all has to be there: celebration, an after-action analysis of what went right and what can be improved next year, and the money!

And there you have it. A goal is valuable, attainable, measurable, committed to memory by everyone involved, a date of attainment, and a burning desire to achieve it. It is supported initially by involving the team in setting the goal so they have ownership in it. You attached rewards to winning and everyone knows what the rewards are. You held everyone accountable to staying engaged in the game and doing the things necessary to win. You led by example and were personally committed to winning and were enthusiastic about it. You took the time to teach your people how to reach the goal and you set guidepost goals along the way that provided both benchmarks and small tastes of victory. You kept a scoreboard and you talked about things in real time with your team. If necessary, you made adjustments along the way to better align your team with the goal. Finally, you provided a celebration when you won, along with a dramatic and meaningful award presentation and a candid after-action review of what you did well that allowed you to win, and some of the things you can work on next year to make even greater gains.

If you're overwhelmed by how much is required in order to first set a true goal and then to keep everyone engaged in achieving it, don't be. You won't be able to do it alone, so don't even try! Include your executive team and make sure they all lead by example as well. Once everyone knows that you're serious about winning, they'll either join you or they'll get out of your way either by their choice or yours.

Here's one more tip, and then we'll end. When your team is setting goals, don't allow the goals to be too easy to hit. Easy goals are worthless. Yes, they need to be attainable, but they need to be challenging. If you set a goal too low, you'll actually insult your superstars. If you set it too high, nobody will want to play. You have to make sure it's just right!

None of this is difficult but it does take time, effort, and passion. You can do it.

I wish you my best.

REVIEW / ACTION STEPS

1. Set a true goal and go for it! Please remember to do the following:

- Involve your team in the process.

- Make sure everyone knows what's in it for them (rewards).

- Once everyone buys into the goal, make it the standard; if people don't own it, they don't belong on your team.

- Lead by example with your own commitment and enthusiasm.

- Invest time teaching people how to win.

- Keep a scoreboard and talk about it all the time.

- Set stepping-stone goals (guideposts) along the way and celebrate each win as they happen.

- Keep your word and pay up!

SUMMARY

If you want to improve your company with lasting transformation, there are a lot of things you need to do. Setting a true goal and then rallying your team around accomplishing it is one of the things you *absolutely* must do in order to bring out the best in your team.

If your goal is meaningful and if you tackle it with vigor and enthusiasm, it will do much to bring unity and synchronicity to your team. It can also be a lot of fun for everyone.

Before we end this chapter, I want to share with you one of the big mistakes I personally made as a business owner. I used to have too many major goals going at the same time.

One year, my company had six true goals that we were going after—all at the same time! Yes, they were all valuable, attainable, and measurable, but they were not committed to memory! Most people could rattle off three, four, or even five of them, but nobody, including me, could remember all six without looking at our notes! (So much for burning desire!) My over-ambition turned out to be counterproductive. There was no focus and we ended up missing every single goal we set, all six.

In our after-action review, everyone said what I was already thinking: There were too many things to focus on at one time and it just caused confusion.

The following year, we had a single goal to go after, and it was a big one. We were all laser focused on it and we talked about it all the time. We trained the ways to achieve it. We had guidepost goals along the way. We made signs (scoreboards) and hung them all over our facilities. Everyone was playing to win, and we did win. As a result, our small business paid out over $80,000 in bonuses that year.

Our celebration was a blast! Our individual team members were rewarded nicely and our team grew closer through the experience. From that year on, we only had one goal per year that we went after. We called it our "Annual Solid Intention."

I encourage you to learn from my mistake. Simple is better. *Laser focus* is required if you're going to meet challenging goals.

Please make sure you own the processes outlined in this white paper and put them to use in your own business. If you can commit to this for one full year, I guarantee you'll never go another day without having a true goal to go after. The results are just too significant to ignore!

I wish you all the best. Go get unstuck!

STRATEGY 10

VISION, MISSION, VALUES STATEMENTS

In an effort to feel good and to pump up the troops, business owners get the idea to write vision, mission, and values statements. The business owner holds a weekend retreat with consultants and his/her executive team to create the most poetic, sweeping statements that will sound wonderful to the team and look great on their marketing material.

The executives come back to work on Monday morning pumped up from the retreat. They have a pizza party in the decorated conference room and enthusiastically tell everyone the deal! The team, hungry for purpose, plans and direction eagerly embraces the "rebirth" of their company. Everyone is excited and proud as the shiny new engraved plaque is hung in the lobby!

But after the last helium-inflated balloon drops on the conference room floor, so too drops the true benefit of this exercise. It usually ends there. The only thing to show for it is the gravestone reminder, which is the dusty spiderweb-covered plaque that was once proudly nailed to the lobby wall. Now it is an inside joke around the water cooler. Bummer.

Your company's vision, mission, and values statements are not intended to be motivational tools; they are management tools. They guide all of the operations in a business. They're used when interviewing new employee candidates. They're referenced when conducting performance reviews. They're considered when making strategic decisions. They determine whether someone is eligible for pay raises and promotions. They define the specific reasons some employees get terminated.

The statements express the standard of how the company will operate and how each individual team member is to conduct him or herself. They provide the rules of how people will treat each other, your customers, your vendors, and your equipment. They clearly define the "personality" of the company and they include the specific goals that the team is going after together. They are the most powerful accountability tool you can develop, if you do it right. Imagine everyone on your team always being on the same page, well, this *is* the page!

People have different definitions of what vision, mission, and values statements are. What some people call "vision," others call "mission." What some people refer to as their "values statement," others claim as their "mission."

To make sure we're on the same page, I'll let you know how I define them. These definitions will remain consistent throughout this entire white paper, but once you get back to your offices, you can call them whatever you'd like!

Vision statement: This is an explanation of why the company exists and what its purpose is. It states the company's long-term objectives and the overall governance and tone of the company. Think of it as a combination of a "who we are," "why we're here," and a "where we're going" statement. A vision statement is "future oriented." It is your company's "declaration."

Mission statement: This statement is a detailed account of the overall strategy and the specific tactics the company will employ in pursuit of the vision. Think of this as the "how we do it" statement. A mission statement is "now" oriented. It is your company's "constitution."

Values statement: This is a detailed listing of all the behavioral rules that will be followed by all individual team members; all of the time. These are the self-imposed laws that are not illegal in the outside world per se, but rules that your team agrees to abide by. It is your company's agreed-upon laws. It clearly defines what behavior is acceptable and what is not.

Ultimately, in order for your vision, mission, and values statements to become real, everyone on your team needs to agree to and buy in to the content of the statements. That means you have to include your team in the development of the statements. But before you do that, you, the business owner, have to write the first draft.

You started the company or you bought it or inherited it. As the chief leader in your company, it is your responsibility to define the outside parameters of who you are, why you exist, what you're going to do, how you'll do it, and your rules. There are a series of questions you have to ask yourself, and then candidly answer, to determine what the outside boundaries are for your company.

I'll provide you with those questions after a brief description of what each of the statements represents. We will begin with the vision statement.

> Vision statement: This is an explanation of why the company exists and what its purpose is. It states the company's long-term objectives and the overall governance and tone of the company. Think of it as a combination of a "who we are," "why we're here" and a "where we're going" statement. It is your company's "declaration."
>
> To assist you in drafting your first vision statement, ask yourself the following questions and write down your honest answers:
>
> - Why did you start (or buy or take over) your company?
>
> - How is your company important to you, your team members, your customers, and your community?
>
> - What does your company do?
>
> - Why makes your company special?
>
> - Why should people want to work at your company?
>
> - Why should your customers buy from you instead of your competitor?

- What are your specific goals?

- Why are those goals important to you?

- Why are your goals important to your team?

- Any other questions you think are important in defining who your company is, why it exists, and what your company is going to accomplish.

As you're asking and answering those questions, please be future oriented. Don't worry about where you are now relative to those questions. Instead, be specific on where you *desire* to be.

Once you've thoughtfully and candidly answered those questions and have written down the answers, you have the content of what should become the first draft of your vision statement! Use the answers you've written down to define who you are (as a company), why you exist, and where you're going. If your company already has a specific goal you're going after together (and I hope you do!), then be sure to include this in your vision statement as one of the answers of where you're going.

As you write the first vision statement draft, please don't worry about being poetic or noble sounding. Don't try to create a masterpiece and don't try to feel like you have to impress anyone with it. Just be genuine in your words. Say what you mean.

Also, don't get hung up on the length of your vision statement draft. It may only be two or three sentences; it might be a full-page long. The length doesn't matter, but the content does.

After you've completed your first draft, please read the draft to yourself and then ask yourself, "Does this vision statement touch me emotionally?" If it does, great! You did it. You've created your vision statement draft that you will bring to your team for their blessing and/or modification. But if your draft did not touch you emotionally, then you have to look at all the answers you gave to the initial questions you asked yourself and for each answer you gave, ask a new question: "Why is my answer important?" You're questioning deeply into your original answers so you can get to the heart of what's truly important to you. Write down the answers and then repeat the process. Use those deeper answers to create a deeper vision statement draft. Do this until you're affected on an emotional level when you read your vision statement draft. When that happens, you've got it! It's time to move on to creating your mission statement draft.

Mission statement: This statement is a detailed account of the overall strategy and the specific tactics the company will employ in pursuit of the vision. Think of this as the "how we do it" statement. A mission statement is "now" oriented. It is your company's "constitution."

Now it's time for you to ask yourself more questions. You'll use your answers to these questions to draft your company mission statement:

- How do we achieve our vision?

- What systems should be referenced?

- Do we have an employee handbook that should be referenced?

- What are our overall operational strategies and our guiding tactics?

- What do our individual team members need to do in order for us to reach our vision?

- What overall philosophies do we need to employ in order for us to reach our vision? (For example, what is our customer service philosophy, our philosophy regarding quality, and our philosophies relative to any and all of our competitive differentiators?)

- What other questions do I need to ask myself in order to answer the bigger question, "How do we do it?"

Once you have these questions answered, look at your answers. Then use the content of your answers to write your mission statement draft. The mission statement draft should end up being a narrative providing the specific answer to the question of how you're going to achieve your vision.

Again, don't worry about form; just concern yourself with function. You want everyone to be crystal clear on specifically how you're going to achieve your vision. It doesn't need to be poetic; you can even use bullet points.

When you've completed this, please read your mission statement and then ask yourself, "If I knew nothing else about my business, does this mission statement specifically and wholly answer the question of how we're going to achieve our vision?" If the answer is yes, then congratulations! You have your mission statement draft. If later you determine that there are other things you're going to do to reach your vision that weren't included in your first draft, simply add them to what you've already created. Do this until you're completely satisfied that you've clearly articulated *specifically* how your company will achieve its vision.

Congratulations. You now know who you are, why you exist, what you're going to do, and how you're going to do it. Now it's time to specify the manner in which your team members will conduct themselves as they execute the mission in pursuit of the vision. It's time to create your company values statement.

Values statement: This is a detailed listing of all the behavioral rules that will be followed by all individual team members, all of the time. These are the self-imposed laws that are not illegal in the outside world per se, but rules that your team agrees to abide by. It is your company's agreed-upon laws. It clearly defines what behavior is acceptable and what is not.

To create the values statement, ask yourself and then answer the following questions:

- What behaviors do we value at (our company)? (Or what behaviors are expected of our team members?)

- What behaviors do we *not* value at (our company)? (Or what behaviors are unacceptable to our company?)

- Specifically, how should our team members treat each other?

- Specifically, how should our team members treat our customers?

- Specifically, how should our team members treat our vendors, our equipment, our cash, and our facility?

- What are the behaviors that I've seen in this company or other companies I've worked at that are unacceptable to me?

- What other values do I hold dear that I want to be laws that guide our company?

Once you've answered these questions, use the answers to create your values statement. Again, don't worry about the form of your statement. Use bullet statements if that's easier and clearer for you to articulate. Your goal is for anyone to be able to read your values statement and know all of the self-imposed rules of behavior that your team is expected to demonstrate all day, every day.

And that's how you do it! By following these procedures, you will be armed with your first draft of your vision, mission, and values statements. Now it's time to get the rest of your team on board.

If your company is small enough that everyone can fit comfortably around a conference table, I suggest you call a meeting to rollout your statements. This isn't a party, it's a working meeting.

Provide a copy of the statements to each of your team members beforehand and let them know that you've created a tool that is going to guide your company. Let them know that this is not a motivational tool, but rather an operational guide that will synchronize your team in pursuing excellence. Let them know that the intention isn't to sound good, it's to define specifically what everyone will be accountable to executing all of the time.

Ask your individual team members to read your thoughts and to make notes on their copy of the draft regarding areas they believe should be added, tweaked, or completely overhauled from what you've suggested. Let them know that the goal of the meeting you've scheduled is to come away from that meeting with an agreed-upon official vision, mission, and values statement that will immediately become the standard that each member of the team, including yourself, will be accountable to on a daily basis.

And then, have the meeting. Start by telling your team what the purpose of each statement is. Then read them your draft and ask them how the draft should be changed to best reflect their own personal feelings and opinions of how things should be.

Encourage your team to speak up and to speak freely and remind everyone that once they agree to it, they'll be accountable to it.

Please let your team know how you intend the statements to be used:

How You Will Use the Statements

- As conversation pieces during interviews.
- To read at the beginning of all formal company meetings to set the tone and to ask if we're living

up to our statements (and honestly answer that question)—and if we're not—to discuss the variation of what we say from what we do and determine how to close that gap.

- During each workday to either compliment or coach people based on their adherence to the content of our statements.

- To be referenced during employee reviews.

- To be considered when deciding on pay raises and promotions.

- To be discussed when counseling someone or terminating his/her employment.

- In making strategic decisions.

- In our marketing and branding campaigns.

- In determining bonuses and awards.

- To be used by everyone on our team to correct wrongs when you see them.

- To guide our actions and decisions.

- To be a promise to every member of this team that the content of our statements will be supported and promoted by the owner and executive team of our company.

Everyone must understand that the vision, mission, and values statements you all just agreed on are not intended to be the final draft. You'll continue to add or change the content as your company grows and as you realize some important factors were initially overlooked that should be in the statements. That said, everyone must be clear that the current vision, mission, and values statements are the standards and it is expected that everyone will execute accordingly.

If your company is too big for everyone to fit around a conference table at the same time, then start by working with your executive team. Do exactly what was just described, but instead of doing it with your entire team, do it with your senior leaders.

Once your senior leadership team has agreed to a vision, mission, and values statement, please provide that draft to your entire team and schedule a company-wide meeting. Ask each member of your team to review the draft and come to the meeting prepared with their suggestions to improve on these statements. And then have the meeting.

The reason you should work with your executive team before having the company-wide meeting is because it will actually save you time by doing this in stages.

Please remember, the tail follows the head. As the head of your company, you have to integrate the vision, mission, and values into everything you do. You have to talk about them every day. When you compliment someone, tie the compliment back to your statements. When you reprimand someone, tie it back to your statements. When your executive team meets, make sure every initiative is tied back to your statements. When you do this, your executive team will follow your lead. When your executive team does this, every team member will do it too. It really does work that way, but it does require constant attention. In other words, you have to talk about it all the time!

In summary, we're not talking about an event. Creating the vision, mission, values is just the beginning. Getting the team's input allows them to take ownership of the statements. But even that is not enough. You have to give the statements teeth and truly make them the standard in everything you do.

It's not easy to do and it requires effort. But the rewards make it worth it. You no longer have to be the police in your company, the statements are. You no longer need to hope people do the right things, the statements make them. You no longer have to be the big boss, the statements are. Your valuable team members no longer need to worry about looking after themselves, the statements are protecting them. Your job just got a lot easier and the people in your company are on the same page. Congratulations!

REVIEW / ACTION STEPS

1. Schedule time to work alone, answering the series of questions asked above, so you'll have the content ideas you want to write in each of your statements.

2. Once you have the answers to those questions, use the content to create your first draft vision, mission, and values statements.

3. Read your draft and ask yourself if the content is meaningful and inspiring to you. If not,

ask yourself why the answers you gave were important to you and add those reasons to your statements (sometimes the why is what excites us most).

4. Once you're satisfied with your draft, schedule a meeting with either your entire team or your executive team with the agenda of considering your vision, mission, and values statements draft and then modifying, improving, and then ultimately adopting an official company vision, mission, and values statement.

5. Provide each of your team members a copy of your draft statements and request that everyone take time to formulate their own ideas of what should be added, taken out, or modified from your draft in preparation for the company or executive team meeting that's been scheduled to formalize the statements.

6. Hold the meeting. Adopt agreed-upon vision, mission, and values statements or schedule a follow-up meeting to finalize your work. Work with your team until you've all agreed on your company's vision, mission, and values statements!

7. Once it's adopted, please make sure you and your team refer to the content of the statements wherever and whenever it can serve the team well. The bulleted points written above (under the heading "How You Will Use the Statements") will give you ideas on how/when to use these statements so that you can "give them teeth."

SUMMARY

This white paper discussed why most company vision, mission, and values statements don't serve any purpose other than to provide a home for spiders. The people that created these statements weren't committed to specificity nor were they committed to making the content of the statements part of the DNA of their companies.

Your team's thoughtful and specific vision statement provides a picture of what you all want your company to look like and what you all want to accomplish.

Your team's thoughtful and specific mission statement provides the strategic and operational framework that explains exactly how you'll get from where you are to where you all want to be.

Your team's thoughtful and specific values statement will provide agreed-upon rules that will guide everyone's behavior. Nothing has to be personal anymore; everyone's expected to follow the same agreed-upon rules all the time, with no exceptions.

But please remember that the creation of these statements is not where the power is. The power comes from using the content of these statements in your everyday operations.

You have to constantly remind people of what you all agreed to. You do this by reading the statements at the beginning of every meeting.

You have to make sure everyone does what they've agreed to. You do this by asking the question after reading the statements, "Are we living up to this?" And you can never just let things go. You have to run a tight ship, and you have to make sure nobody wavers from your promises.

You have to make sure that every time you correct someone's behavior, you tie it back to the statements. One of my favorite things to do instead of correcting people is to ask them if what they're doing (that I'm not happy with) is in accordance with the vision, mission, or values and if so, to please show me. When you do this, self-correction takes place!

When you compliment someone, tie it back to the statements. Pay raises, promotions, terminations, new hires, strategic decisions, tactical decisions, tie them all back to your statements. If you want your team to take the statements seriously, then you must show them how seriously you take them by talking about them constantly.

I know this may sound like a lot of work and it is. But once you get the statements into the fiber of your company and in the veins of your team members, it will become much easier and the rewards make it all worthwhile. This really does work, but only if you do the work.

I wish you all my best. Go get unstuck!

STRATEGY 11

THE GREAT HUDDLE

What is a Great Huddle? It's a staff meeting! But it's not your normal run-of-the-mill type of staff meeting. Instead, it's a meaningful meeting where your team will (1) realign themselves to your vision, mission, and values. Then (2) they'll each have an opportunity to speak so that everyone gets to know each other on a deeper level. Following that, (3) you or a member of your executive team will give a leadership briefing, which includes the specific things you and your executive team are working on and the reasons behind it. You'll share critical financial numbers with your team so that everyone is more in tune with the state of your company (for better or for worse). And you'll give an update on where your company stands relative to your goals. Then, (4) someone will give a brief "lesson in leadership" or will provide refresher "standard operating procedure" training to your team. And finally, (5) you'll cap off this meeting with an awards presentation to recognize superior achievement from within your ranks.

We'll cover each of these sections in this white paper, but first, I have to give credit where credit is due! I didn't make up the name The Great Huddle. It came from an outstanding book I've read at least a few times over the past several years. The book is *The Great Game of Business*, written by Jack Stack. It's a fantastic book and one of your action steps is to get that book and read it. I can tell you that I've personally used many of the ideas presented in *The Great Game of Business*, and while I can't specifically quantify the exact amount of profit and company value I've gained as a result of reading the book and taking action, I know I've benefitted tremendously. You'll learn about the powerful benefits of "open book management" and specifically how you can use your company financials to build a smart, well-informed, effective, committed team of people.

Now we'll discuss each of the elements stated above that will be the content of your Great Huddles.

VISION/MISSION/VALUES

Start each meeting by reading your vision, mission, and values statements. After each statement is read, ask your team, "Are we living up to this?" Encourage everyone to answer that question candidly.

When you ask that question, sometimes the answer will be, "Yes, we're living up to it." But other times, there will be certain elements of your statements that are not being lived up to.

If it is the latter, then please ask everyone, "What are we going to change, our behavior or our statements?" Without congruency of actions, your vision/mission/values statements are worthless. If what you say about how your team will work together (in your statements) is different than how your team is actually working together, then something is wrong; either your statements are wrong or the behavior is wrong. And of course, if something is wrong, then it needs to be fixed! So give your team the opportunity to decide for themselves what needs to change: their behavior or the statements.

For example, let's suppose that part of your values statement reads, "Gossiping is destructive and shouldn't be tolerated." But at your Great Huddle, it was exposed that there is gossiping going on. Before you address the issue of gossiping, first ask the question, "Do we want to change our values statement to allow for gossiping, or should we address the fact that we say we won't gossip but aren't currently living up to it?"

99.99% of the time, your team will want to change any behavior that is not in line with your statements. It's very rare that you'll ever have someone suggest you lower a standard to match your current behavior! Once everyone agrees that the values statement is correct and the behavior needs to change, you can address specifically how you're going to fix it. And the beauty is, you aren't the police, the statements are! That means you can objectively facilitate the corrections. It's not personal!

By starting your Great Huddle with reading your vision/mission/values and then sincerely asking if the team is living up to it, you give the statements meaning. When people know that their behavior is accountable to the statements, they'll take the statements much more seriously and that's the purpose.

So start each Great Huddle by (1) reading the vision/mission/values, and then (2) asking everyone if we're living up to it (and encouraging their candid opinions), and then (3) letting the team decide what needs to change: the statements or the behavior, and finally, (4) going through the process of addressing the things that need to be corrected so that moving ahead, your team's behavior will match the content of your statements. Note: if you don't currently have a company vision/mission/values document, please go to white paper 10 and get on it!

STATE OFS

You can call this section of the Great Huddle anything you'd like, but in my experience we called it State Ofs. You've heard of the State of the Union address that the president of the United States gives periodically. Well, this is the State of Themselves address that each person will give! In short, I call them State Ofs.

This is where you go around the room and everyone gets to stand up and talk about anything they'd like to for however long you give them. To determine how long you're going to give each person, start by considering the total amount of minutes you want to dedicate to this portion of your meeting and then divide that number by the amount of people in the room. For example, if you're willing to invest thirty minutes total in doing State Ofs and you have ten people in the room, then everyone gets three minutes to do their individual State

Ofs. People should feel free to take less time than that, but they all need to be held to three minutes max.

During State Ofs, people can talk about things going on in their personal lives (such as buying a house or a new car, having a baby, going on vacation, etc.). They can also take this time to personally and publicly thank certain people on the team who have provided exceptional support to the person talking. The person can talk about projects being worked on, or recent accomplishments, or anything else. The purpose of State Ofs is to get people to know each other better and for everyone to have a chance to speak to everyone about anything they deem important either personally or professionally. This is also a great opportunity for people to know what other people on the team are working on.

For larger organizations, you should ask people to start their State Ofs by introducing themselves, telling everyone what they do at your company, and how long they've been employed at your company. This will help people learn each other's names and will help people know who does what at your company.

When you do State Ofs, some people will be shy and won't say much. Other people will use it as an opportunity to show everyone how funny they are. Others will be reluctant to share personal info and will stick to keeping it professional. Still others will only share personal info and won't talk about business. My suggestion is to let them be themselves and give them their time. State Ofs can be a lot of fun, and over time, your team will get to know each other much better than if you skip doing this.

LEADERSHIP BRIEFING

You may choose to do this section of the Great Huddle yourself or you may choose to have different members of your executive team take turns giving the leadership briefing. Either is okay, but remember, your job is to develop your leaders and when you give them the opportunity to run this section of your Great Huddles you will provide them valuable leadership experience. For that reason, I suggest you have the other leaders in your company facilitate this section of the Great Huddle.

During your leadership briefings, the following areas should be covered:

- A report on the specific things the executive team is working on and the reasons behind it.

- A briefing of the critical financial numbers so that everyone is more in tune with the state of your company (for better or for worse).

- An update on where your company stands relative to your goals.

When your team knows specifically what you and your executive team are working on, they won't need to speculate. Instead, they'll understand what you're doing, why you're doing it, and will be on the lookout to help you achieve your objectives. In doing this, you're also preventing an "us and them" mentality that often times divides "management and staff." People are empowered when they know what's going on and they're also more connected. Remember, every person on your team is responsible for different pieces of the puzzle, and by sharing strategy and tactics with them, you're giving them the benefit of knowing what the puzzle is supposed to look like as they work with the different puzzle pieces each day.

What are your critical numbers? Again, I strongly urge you to read *The Great Game of Business*, by Jack Stack. In short, your critical numbers are the numbers that most relate to your goals. For example, if one of your goals is centered on annual net profits, then a critical number to report each month is where your company stands year-to-date in net profits. If one of your goals includes paying off your line of credit, then a critical number to report each month is the total balance remaining on the line of credit.

This is where many business owners start to get uncomfortable. Sharing the financials seems dangerous to them. In my career, I've been told that my "financials sharing" was "stupid." And yet, the result from sharing the financials with my team has proven anything but stupid!

When people know the numbers, they know the score. When people know the score, they become more involved. It fuels their competitive spirits and makes things real instead of just being conceptual. When you talk about your specific numbers with your team, you should teach them specifically how to make those numbers better. You want your team members to be engaged and passionate about making your company stronger, don't you? Well, how can they do that if they don't know where you stand relative to where you all want to go? The answer is obvious; they can't know! So what's the downside of sharing your numbers?

Once you've given your team an update on the executive team initiatives and you've shared the financials, you have to be sure that you tie it all back to any company goals you're all going after together. Please don't leave it to your team to connect the dots. Instead, talk specifically about how the initiatives and the numbers relate to your goal(s).

Use this time to teach your team how to reach your goal. For example, if your goal is to earn a net profit of 10 percent this year, let people know specifically how the executive team initiatives are helping to achieve this. Suppose your executive team is working on updating your initial training program for new hires. Be sure to explain to your team specifically how that initiative will help you earn higher net profits (prevents costly mistakes, enhances efficiency, reduces costly turnover, training is completed more quickly by being regimented, and all of the other ways in which that initiative helps to drive net profits).

You've already shared the critical numbers with your team (in this example, it would be year-to-date net profit margin). Now it's time to brainstorm with your team on either (1) how to close the gap between where you are and where you want to be or (2) if you're on pace or ahead of pace for hitting your goal, use this time to talk about what you're doing right that's allowed you to be on the path to success.

By the time this section of the Great Huddle comes to an end, you've (1) reviewed your vision/mission/ values and your team has taken the time to hold themselves accountable to the statements. (2) Everyone on your team has stood up and given their own personal State Of. And (3) everyone has been briefed on what the executive team is focusing on, what initiatives are underway and how the business is performing relative to your financials and your goals. Now it's time for some team-member development!

LESSON IN LEADERSHIP / STANDARD OPERATING PROCEDURE TRAINING

How many companies actually take the time to teach their team members how to be strong leaders? You'd think that since building leadership depth in an organization is so important that most businesses would do it, but the sad fact of the matter is, they don't.

Instead, business owners take for granted that by the time most people reach adulthood they already know about leadership traits and characteristics. These owners don't recognize that refresher training is critical in helping people stay focused on doing the right things. Many business owners never had any formal leadership training themselves, so perhaps they wouldn't even know where to begin. I'll help you with that.

When preparing for giving a lesson in leadership, choose a leadership trait or characteristic that you appreciate and admire. Examples are: leadership by example, integrity, attention to detail, servant leadership, leaders as teachers, discipline, commitment, technical competence, candor, being visionary, being strategic, being compassionate, remaining objective, being supportive or any other leadership characteristic you can think of (or find by searching about leadership on your favorite Internet search engine).

Once you choose the specific topic, plan a brief presentation about the characteristic or trait and be sure to tie it back to your specific business.

For example, if you choose to talk about attention to detail, first talk about it in general terms relative to why great leaders pay strict attention to detail. But then bring it back to your own company by giving real-life examples of how attention to detail differentiates your team from your competitors. Or talk specifically about how a lack of attention to detail costs your company profits, profit margin, customers, reputation, and sales.

Don't worry about delivering an earth-shattering presentation that will have angels singing a chorus of halleluiahs! You don't have to discover some unknown truth about leadership that will instantly transform your people into enlightened warriors. You just have to remind people of the importance of those characteristics or traits and you have to bring it into the business by tying those ideas into your specific company operations. Sure, some people may learn a thing or two, but for most people, this will be important refresher training and will refocus them on why it's important to do what you know.

On alternating Great Huddles, you can choose to invest this time providing standard operating procedure or SOP training instead of giving a lesson in leadership. If you've recently developed a new system or updated an old one, this is a great time to make sure everyone on your team is clear on it. Or maybe you've had errors or waste lately because a particular procedure isn't being followed. This is a great time to correct that. If there have been changes to your employee handbook, this would be a great time to discuss it with your team.

The purpose of this portion of your Great Huddle is for your people to learn. It can be refresher training, new training, leadership training, systems training, HR training, or whatever other type of training you think will be valuable to your team members and/or your company.

Here's a final tip for this portion of your Great Huddle: Don't do it alone. Ask for volunteers to conduct this portion of the training. You can let them know what the topic will be or you can ask them to come up with it themselves. Be sure you give them time to prepare their presentation and mandate that they take it seriously. But then give them the opportunity to own the stage and for your team to hear perspectives other than your own. This will take pressure off you from having to plan all the training and will simultaneously give your individual team members the opportunity to refine their own leadership abilities.

AWARDS

When was the last time you received formal recognition for your great results? How did it make you feel? Did you get a certificate, a trophy, a plaque, or any other tangible symbol of accomplishment? Did you take it home and show it to loved ones? Did it inspire you with renewed enthusiasm and commitment? How did you feel about the person or organization that recognized your achievement? Did you feel a stronger bond with them? Were you appreciative? Did the award make you proud of yourself for your hard work and achievement? Sure it did!

We all know the wonderful power of awards, but how many business owners invest time each month in giving awards to recognize outstanding effort and/or results? If you're in the minority of business owners that do present awards regularly, then great for you! You already know firsthand the many benefits that come with awards. If you're in the majority of business owners that do not give awards regularly, then you have a fantastic opportunity in front of you! (Yes, you should put this on your Opportunities List, discussed in White Paper 2.)

A great way to end each Great Huddle is by having an awards presentation. There are many different ways to do this, and it's up to you to decide which way is best for your company.

Start by determining what the criteria for winning the monthly award will be. Are you going to base it on productivity, effort, alignment with your vision/ mission/values, or some other criteria?

Who will choose the award winner each month? Will you (the owner) do it yourself, or will you have a vote within the executive team? Who will present the award at the Great Huddle? As you're thinking this through, please consider that giving an award is often times just as rewarding as getting an award, so don't hog all the glory for yourself! Let other people make the award presentation *at least* some of the time.

One thing that surprised me as a business owner was when we created an award where the winner of the award got to choose the winner of next month's award and then he/she was able to present it to the winner. That became our most cherished award!

I thought that the award that was chosen by the executive team each month would be the major award and that the team member to team member award would be a nice, but secondary award. That didn't turn out to be the case! Instead, the award that was chosen and presented from teammate to teammate became the most prestigious award! I strongly suggest you consider creating an award like that.

Then decide what the award will be. Will you give a plaque, trophy, certificate, gift card, cash, parking spot, or an extra day off as the award, or do you have something else in mind? One of my companies gave an old combat boot that was spray-painted with metallic gold paint as our monthly award. I know it sounds ridiculous, but it was quite an honor to receive it! As my company became more mature and was generating large profits, I changed the boot for a very nice plaque. I thought my team would appreciate that change, but they didn't! They wanted the boot back (and yes, the boot came back). The point is, you don't have to go overboard in choosing what to give as an award. You just have to do it.

Another fun thing to do when creating the award is to name the award after one of your very top leaders who has had a long track record of greatness within your company.

Once you determine who will choose the winner, what criteria will be used, what the award will be, and who will present the award, you're ready to go! But please make sure your awards are most meaningful and beneficial by making sure that as the awards are presented, you provide very specific reasons *why* the person is being awarded.

When you make it specific, people get to learn from other people's successes. Furthermore, the award is nice to receive, but the specific acknowledgment of the great contributions the person made is even more meaningful to the recipient. Don't slack in this. Don't just announce who won the award. Take your time, be precise, and use this as a teachable moment for your other team members. By all means, tie your presentation back to your vision/mission/values.

When the person accepts the award, please give that individual the opportunity to give a short acceptance speech. When you do this, you give the award winner the opportunity to thank other people on the team and the opportunity to share their feelings and reinforce the values of your company.

And there you have it: The Great Huddle!

The Great Huddle is your highly effective staff meeting full of learning, bonding, alignment, and recognition. Here are a few more tips, and then we'll end: First, please schedule your Great Huddle to be on the same day and same time each month. For example, "From 6:00 p.m. to 7:30 p.m. on the first Wednesday of each month." That way, people can easily schedule their lives around your Great Huddles.

The next tip is to be sure to schedule this meeting outside of your normal business hours. The last thing you want is for the phone to be ringing, deadlines to be pressing, and people anxious to get out of the meeting to handle their day-to-day operations. By having it after normal working hours, people can relax and be focused during the meeting.

Since you're going to have this meeting after normal business hours, you'll be cutting into dinnertime for many people. So you'll have to feed them! Oftentimes, these meetings will force you to pay overtime wages for non-exempt employees. That's okay! Do it. If you run your Great Huddles as suggested and you put thought and planning into making each meeting meaningful, the return on investment of your time, money, and effort far outweigh the cost of food, awards, and overtime pay.

It's not easy, but it is fun. It's not cheap, but it is meaningful. Go ahead and give it a try. And please feel free to make any adjustments you think are beneficial along the way.

I wish you all my best!

REVIEW / ACTION STEPS

1. Please get the book, *The Great Game of Business* by Jack Stack and read it!

2. Either adopt or modify the following recurring agenda for your Great Huddles:

Great Huddle Agenda

I. Vision/Mission/Vision: Read it and then hold your team's behavior accountable to it.

II. State Ofs: Everyone has a specified amount of time to talk about themselves, their work, thank other people, and/or let everyone know what they're currently working on.

III. Leadership Briefing: Includes:

- A report on the specific things you and your executive team are working on and the reasons behind it.

- Sharing the critical financial numbers with your team so that everyone is more in tune with the state of your company (for better or for worse).

- Update on where your company stands relative to your goals.

IV. Lesson in Leadership/ Standard Operating Procedure Training: You or a member of your team will either give a lesson in a particular leadership trait or characteristic or someone on your team will provide procedural training.

V. Awards: Where specific achievement is recognized (and tied back to the vision/ mission/values).

3. Create your Great Huddle schedule and distribute to your team.

4. Execute your own Great Huddles!

SUMMARY

When your company staff meetings are informative, interesting, engaging, enjoyable, and rewarding, your team members will look forward to them. They'll be productive meetings, and the result can be a substantial return on your investment of time, energy, and effort.

Your Great Huddles will provide a forum for reinforcing your vision, mission, and values statements. They will provide everyone the opportunity to get to know each other on an even deeper level both professionally and personally. Speculation and rumors will be replaced with informed team members who feel included in the company's strategic initiatives. Your team members will learn or be reminded in how to become stronger leaders. Your company communications regarding systems and procedures will be enhanced. Finally, people will be formally and publicly recognized for their great contributions.

Once you experience the benefits of the Great Huddle, you'll never understand why most businesses either don't have staff meetings at all or have the typical brain-deadening staff meetings, which are dreaded and resented by everyone.

The Great Huddle is a powerful team-building and company-building event and it's a fantastic tool in building an exceptionally strong company culture.

It's not easy and it does require time and money. But it is fun and it does work.

I wish you all my best as you get unstuck!

STRATEGY 12

SYSTEMS THROUGH STANDARD OPERATING PROCEDURES

Think about this for a minute: If you have people in your company that are doing the same job, but each person is doing it differently, then only one person (at the most) is doing it the *best* way. Everyone else is doing it in a less-efficient and less-profitable manner.

Compounding that, when people do the same job in different ways, it is likely you'll have a wide range of variation in your products or services. As we all know, variation can kill your brand and frustrate your customers.

A key in running efficient, profitable operations is to have systems that everyone follows in producing your product or delivering your services. The goal is to develop systems that promote the highest level of efficiency and profitability while producing predictability in outcomes. In other words, you need to determine the best way your products can be produced or your services delivered and make that the *standard* that everyone will follow.

Once your systems are created, they must be written down in a procedures manual. This is important for a couple reasons. First, by having them in writing, you can use the manual as a tool in training your team and for accountability purposes. Second, by having a procedures manual or operations manual, your company value increases. Any time a new owner is provided a cookie-cutter approach to running your business, it is more valuable to that person than buying a company and then having to figure out how to operate the business.

Once your systems are documented, your team needs to be trained (or retrained) so everyone knows what the procedures are and understands how to follow the procedures. Then, everyone needs to be held accountable to (1) following the procedures at all times and (2) continuously being on the lookout for opportunities to improve on the existing procedures.

Okay, so far, this is all pretty obvious and you probably haven't learned anything. It's obvious that identifying the best way to do something is important to increase efficiency and profitability. It's obvious that having those best practices (systems) in writing is important for training, accountability, and in increasing company value. It's also obvious that customers want predictability when they purchase your product or service. Without a doubt, you have to develop procedures in order to accomplish this and those procedures need to be taught to your team members. And once trained, of course you have to ensure your team is actually following the procedures you developed and also to look for areas the current procedures can be improved upon to promote additional and ongoing efficiency, profitability, and predictability. There's nothing earth-shattering in any of that. But let me ask you: do you have written procedures in every aspect of your business? Do you ever have problems that repeat themselves? Do all of your team members produce the same quality of work in the same amount of time? Are your procedures periodically reviewed and updated? Do you have formal training for new hires and refresher training for existing team members centered on systems?

If you have a production department, does everyone in that department produce your products the same way? Do they all understand how to use the features on your equipment the same way? Do they all have the same level of speed and accuracy when producing your products? Do you track each person's speed and accuracy? If you do track it, what do you do with that information? Do you have stated standards regarding speed and accuracy of production? Does everyone know what those standards are? Are all of your team members meeting those standards?

Is your production area set up the way it is because you've just organically grown into the current set-up, or have you thoughtfully planned the layout of your production floor to support maximum efficiency? Do people have easy (and fast) access to production supplies, or do they have to leave their work stations to go get supplies from the other side of the production floor?

What about product returns? Do you have a standard of acceptability and are you meeting it? Why are your customers returning products? Do you have to rerun projects due to either not following the customer specs or due to shabby workmanship?

What about your scheduling department? Do they have procedures? How do they determine that deadlines can be met? Do you ever miss deadlines? If so, do you know why? If you know why, have you created a procedure to make sure that you never miss deadlines again? Is it written down? Is everyone trained in it? Are they doing it?

How about your sales department? Do you have a standard sales model that each of your sales reps follows? Are the standards measured and tracked? Are people held accountable to meeting those standards?

Has one of your customers ever complained of making a repeat order and not getting the same thing they ordered the first time around? For example, price variation, delivery variation, quality variation, invoicing variation, or any other variation? Why did this happen? Most importantly, what can you do (specifically) to make sure that never happens again?

If you're in the service business, does every customer encounter have the same feel to it? Do you offer the same level of service to every customer, every day? What service failures seem to happen repeatedly? Are there any typical customer complaints?

I could go on and on (and I suggest you do) asking these types of questions for each department within your company. In most privately held businesses, we have procedures in several areas of our business, but not all. Some systems may be written, some may not be. Most of our people follow the procedures most of the time, but perhaps not all the people all of the time. It is also common to see systems developed, but not formally improved upon even as your company grows. Your old systems may have actually become inefficient as your business has changed.

So how do you go about either creating systems in your business or updating your current systems? The best way to do that is by involving the people who are expected to follow each system in the creation or the updating of those systems. Have each department head get his/her entire team together to answer the following questions:

- Are we all doing things the same way?

- Are we all operating the best way?

- How can we improve our efficiency?

- How can we eliminate waste?

- How can we eliminate variation?

- How can we improve our profitability?

- What are we doing that we shouldn't be doing?

- What aren't we doing what we should be doing?

- What errors occur in this department?

- When an error occurs is it because we don't have a system, or because the system wasn't followed, or was it because we have the wrong system in place?

- If you were in charge of creating the best systems in this department, what would be the first thing you'd fix?

- Are all of our systems in writing?

- Are people held accountable to following our systems?

- How often are our systems improved upon?

- What's the procedure for updating a system?

- Are the updates in writing?

- Is everyone being trained on the updates?

- Is everyone held accountable to following the new, updated systems?

- Who would like the job of creating an operations manual for the entire department? (Maybe this is your department leader or maybe it's someone else in that department who is better at writing.)

You may be very surprised with answers you hear in these meetings. You may also be very pleased with the ideas for improving your efficiency, reducing or eliminating variation, and ultimately, increasing the profitability and value of your company.

As the business owner, it is *not* your job to create the systems yourself. It is not your responsibility to document the systems and create a procedural manual. But it is ultimately *your* responsibility to make sure that those things get done appropriately.

One final point: Don't be overwhelmed if you currently don't have any written systems in your business or if your systems are stale. Just work with your team to create a list of systems that need to be created or updated and then prioritize the list. Once that's done, start knocking them out one by one. It won't happen overnight, but that's okay. Remember the question: "How do you eat an elephant?" Answer: "One bite at a time." The same is true with creating your company's operations manual. "How do you create your company's operations manual?" Answer: "One system at a time."

Please just get going on it and stay on it until it is done. The results will be well worth your effort.

REVIEW / ACTION STEPS

1. Meet with each of your department heads individually and ask them about the procedures in their departments. You may even want to ask them to read this white paper and then have a discussion about the importance of either developing systems, documenting them, training them, or improving on the systems you currently have in place.

2. Have your department heads lead departmental meetings and to ask the questions that are bullet-pointed in this chapter. Please be sure you attend these meetings, but if you have department leaders, let them run the meetings.

3. Have each department make a list of every system they need to either create or update and put in writing. Then, ask them to prioritize the list. And finally, ask them to start working it and

ask them for deadlines in completing each of the new or improved systems (or give them the deadlines yourself).

4. As each system is created and written, please be sure that every team member is properly trained in executing the procedures.

5. As each system is written, please be sure to include them in the correct section of your company's Operations Manual. The Ops Manual is a compilation of all of the systems tabbed by each department within your company.

SUMMARY

When everyone is doing things the same way—the best way—your efficiencies and profitability will be enhanced. Variation in your products or services will be reduced or totally eliminated. The result will be happy customers who will continue to buy from you, thereby further increasing your profitability.

By having written systems in every department within your company, you will increase the value of your company. A company operations manual is tremendously valuable to potential successors of your business.

If you want to operate as efficiently as possible, if you want to eliminate variation and strengthen your brand, if you want to increase the value of your company, then you must have systems and these systems must be documented and continuously updated.

You also have to make sure your team is trained and following the systems. Mandate that they follow the systems to the letter, but at the same time ask them to be on the lookout to make the systems even better and take those ideas to the department leader.

Every time a mistake happens in your company, be sure you determine if the mistake was caused by not having a system, or because someone was not following the system, or because your existing system needs to be reworked. And once you know the reason for the mistake, you have to ensure that appropriate measures are taken to prevent that mistake from happening again.

Please remember to include your team in the development of your systems and in maintaining the different sections in your company's operating manual. Your job isn't to do all the work, but it is your job to make sure the work gets done!

It's not easy and it's a continual process. But with your commitment to systematize your business, documenting your systems, and improving your systems, you'll be doing much to improve the profitability and value of your business. It's well worth the hard work!

Go get unstuck! I wish you all my best!

STRATEGY 13

PERSONAL EFFECTIVENESS

Think about how happy you are in your personal life. Think about your work, your hobbies, your faith, your family, your education, your personal relationships, your dreams and goals, and think about your general state of being.

Now think about your habits, behaviors, and the ways you spend your time. As you think about these things, ask yourself, "Are my thoughts and behaviors congruent with my values?" "Do I think about or behave in ways that are counter to my own well-being?" "How might I occasionally seek temporary pleasure at the cost of true happiness?"

Please take a few minutes and reflect on all that is written above.

Now that you've had some time to think about it, ask yourself this question: "Am I living the life I truly want to live or have I just become accustomed to the life I'm living?" If the answer is that you are not living the life you dreamed of and are in a rut of accepting your life as it is, please know that you're not alone. In fact, most people have incongruences in their lives. Here's why:

There are constant dynamics in your life that require your time, energy, focus, and even require sacrifice from you. We live in an interdependent world and chances are you have people who depend on you to have their own needs or wants met. You have different emotions that affect you during each day. Some are good emotions; others are painful. You probably find yourself pulled in many directions throughout each day. Some of the things you do each day are by design (your choice) while other things are imposed on you.

As a business owner, you're constantly looking to serve all of the different constituencies that you depend on and who depend on you. These constituencies include your spouse, your kids (young or old), your friends, your employees, your customers, your vendors, the bank, the government, and the guy who just pulled out in front of you while you were driving to work! Everyone is always looking to you for help, support, love, time, money, and energy. This can be physically, mentally, and emotionally exhausting at times, but it is part of life and there is no way for a responsible person to avoid it.

After you give so much time, energy, and emotion to meeting your responsibilities (and other peoples' needs), there is little left of yourself to give yourself.

You may choose to fill these precious "you" moments by relaxing and unwinding, trying to recharge your battery. Or you may take advantage of that time to do something fun and entertaining for yourself. Those are great things to do and you should do them. But here's the problem:

After each day is done, you go to sleep and in the morning, you're right back at it again! You're back in "serving others"' mode and the cycle continues to repeat itself. All that is fine, but one thing is missing: the thing that's missing is taking time to *intentionally* plan for and live the life you dreamed of.

Instead, most days are filled with being reactionary instead of intentional. And that is why when people take inventory of their lives, they often find that they aren't living it the way they truly want to. Sometimes, these people have even completely lost themselves. Let me assure you again, this is very common. And the great news is that you can fix it without having to make radical changes.

Before I give you a strategy to try for yourself, let me remind you that personal development is not an event. It is an ongoing process of one smart step after another. It's not realistic to try to do too much at one time because there are just too many things that can and will get in your way. So as you're looking to develop yourself, please be satisfied with each of the many small daily steps you will take because each one is a victory in and of itself. After several days, weeks, then months of doing this, your own personal development and intentionally living will become the new normal for you and your internal peace and happiness will continually grow.

What I'll give you now is a simple strategy for living intentionally. It won't require a lot of time or effort, but will require *daily* attention. Here it is:

Step 1: Take out a blank piece of paper and write the words:

Physical

Mental

Emotional

Spiritual

Relational

Next to each of those words, make a list of all the ways you consider yourself happy. For example, if you have a healthy diet then next to the word "Physical," write, "Healthy diet."

Once you have written all of the things you're happy about in each of the five areas, please write down all of the things you wish were different. Specifically, what are you either doing or not doing that is standing in your way of having complete happiness in each of those areas?

Congratulations! You have just completed your "opportunities list" in each of the areas of your life relative to your physical, mental, emotional, spiritual, and relational health and happiness!

Now, please go back through each of those areas and determine which *single* area of happiness-development can have the most dramatic impact on your overall happiness today. The reason you're picking just one is because transformation takes constant attention and you don't want to overwhelm yourself trying to make too many changes at one time.

Once you have your top priority determined, please look at all of the positive things you identified that are going well for you in that area and please recommit to yourself that you'll keep doing them. Also, be sure to allow yourself self-congratulations for the things you are doing that *are* congruent with your own values and goals. It's not easy to do anything with all the other noise that surrounds your life, and it's important you recognize and appreciate yourself for the things you are doing to make yourself happy.

Now look at all of the things that are not on track in your top priority area of happiness development and determine the single most important thing you want to fix first.

For example, if the top priority area of your happiness development is in the area of spirituality, and the top area you determined as getting in your way of complete happiness in this area of your life is, "I haven't prayed in months," then that is the thing you're now ready to take action on!

As another example, if the top priority area of your happiness development is in the area of physical health and the top problem you identified in this area is that you're overweight, then that is the one thing you're now ready to take action on.

If you've followed these instructions, you have identified the single most important area in your life (physical, mental, emotional, spiritual, or relational) which if developed (improved) can have the biggest impact on your own happiness. You also chose the single thing in that bigger area that can have the most profound impact on your overall happiness in that area. This is a big deal! After all, "A problem identified *is* a problem solved!"

Now I'd like you to ask yourself the following questions:

1. What is the problem I'm looking to solve? (Example answer: I'm looking to become happier in my life in the area of physical health first by committing to lose weight in a healthy way.)

2. Why is it important to my own happiness that I solve this problem?

3. What are the negative ramifications this problem is having on my life (be specific)?

4. What are the implications of those ramifications?

5. How will my life be different when I solve this problem?

6. How else will my life be different?

7. What are all the things I can do that will solve this problem?

8. What is the most important solution to tackle first?

9. What action step(s) can I take in the next seven days that will be steps directly toward solving your problem and becoming happier? (Please be sure you do not overwhelm yourself. Just identify one or two things you can do that you are certain you can do within the next seven days.)

10. Make a list of all the things that may get in your way of being able to complete your action step(s) for the next seven days.

11. Next to each of the things identified in step 10, write your plan on how you'll address each of those things if they come up so that you will complete your weekly action step(s).

12. Now go back and revisit your answers to questions 1 thru 5 above, and then ask yourself, "Am I working on the right thing for the right reasons and is this the most important thing I can do to make myself a happier person?" If the answer is no, then please repeat this entire process. If the answer is yes, then look at your action step(s) and ask yourself if those truly are the best things you should be doing within the next week to move yourself toward happiness in this important area in your life. If the answer to that question is, "Yes, this is the most important thing for me this week," then you're ready to go! You did it!

13. Final step: Complete your action steps! Please understand that nothing happens until there's action. You must be sure you complete your weekly action step(s). Don't overthink it: Just do it! (my gratitude to Nike for "getting it!").

There's nothing magical about this process, but it works every time it's done all the way through. I want to reiterate that when you determine your action steps, *please do not ever overwhelm yourself.* You may even want to break your tactics down into smaller steps. For example, if the top problem you want to solve is the fact that you're overweight and the top thing you want to address is to stop eating ice cream every day, you may want to commit to having ice cream only four times this week instead of seven. If you try to do too much too soon, your chances of success diminish. Please make it manageable for yourself. "Life" is going to happen to you this week, but that can't stop you from living intentionally!

If you revisit this process each and every week, you will transform your life. It will not happen quickly, but it will happen progressively and the changes you make will be lasting changes. The result will be an incremental increase in your overall happiness as a person.

If this all sounds too simplistic, then I'm glad. It's supposed to be simple because simple works. It's supposed to be slow because going slow is much faster than screaming out of the gate only to get frustrated and run back to your old ways. You know this is true because we've all done it!

You have a business plan for your business. You have vision, mission, and values statements for your company. You have goals and you track them. You have systems that guide your behavior. You do SWOT analysis to determine your company strengths, weaknesses, opportunities, and threats and you use the results of those to either make plans or adjust your plans. You spend time and effort deliberately planning for your business development. Now it's time for you to do the same for your own personal development and live the life you want to live. It's time for you to live intentionally!

I wish you all the best in your life and for you to be as happy as you can be.

THE "NOT-SO-SMART" THINGS I'VE DONE OR SEEN
(YES, THAT'S MY STORY AND I'M STICKING TO IT.)

Here they are:

1. It is not so smart to grow faster than your ability to pay for the investment in growth. How do profitable companies go out of business? They run out of cash. The cash may be tied up in accounts receivables, inventory, equipment, building expansion, software upgrades, finance charges, or anywhere else. Fast-growing companies spend a lot of cash to fund that growth. Don't make the mistake of thinking that a profit on your income statement equals an ability to borrow what you need to float cash. At some point, banks just won't lend to you anymore. If you aren't generating enough cash to cover your expenses and repay debt, then you won't get a loan. It's that simple. Please pay attention to cash. If you have to grow a bit more slowly in order to preserve cash, it is smart to do

that. If you can't fathom the idea of slowing your growth, then please just make sure you have the money to fund that growth before you spend it. Or you just may successfully grow yourself out of business.

2. It is not so smart to promote someone to a position they aren't qualified for. Sometimes, we make the mistake of thinking that the best person to promote is the person who is the best in his/her current position. For example, if we need a sales manager, we think that promoting our best sales representative is a good idea. Or if we need a production manager, we think that promoting our best machine operator is the best decision. But in doing this, we can end up turning a super star into a former employee. The talents needed to be in a leadership position are different than the talents required in doing other jobs. Just because someone is great at what he/she is doing does not mean that person will be great in a new position. If you have a management or leadership position open up but don't have a strong leadership candidate in your ranks to take that position, then it is better to look outside of your company and bring someone in. Don't just give the job to the best person you can find within your company. Otherwise, you'll end up ruining a person's career at your company by promoting them to a position he was never qualified for. And it's very hard to demote people, especially if you promoted them with

pay raises. It's more likely you'll just lose them. So don't short cut this. Make sure you promote people who you think have the characteristics necessary to excel in the new position; don't just take someone that's great at what they're doing and think they can do anything.

3. It is not so smart to be the smartest person in the room. The smartest people seek to employ people who are smarter than themselves. The not-so-smartest people are those who are threatened by smarter people. Any time I've ever met a business owner who employs people smarter than the owner, I know the company is valuable, profitable, and a joy to work in! Enough said.

4. It is not so smart to keep people on your team that commit a values violation. If you have a person who lies, cheats, steals, or commits a major values violation, you have to get rid of them. Otherwise, you won't have the moral authority to terminate anyone else who gets silly later on. We all know that it is impossible for good apples to fix a rotten apple, but rotten apples do have the ability to ruin good apples. Don't mess with this. People need to understand that a major values violation equals termination, no exceptions.

5. It is not so smart to keep customers who don't let you earn a profit. Have you ever noticed that some people's idea of fair is when you don't earn

a profit? I'm sure these are very nice people who have their own company's best interest in mind, but if you run a for-profit company, then you can't keep them. They'll suck up your resources, they'll be the biggest complainers and energy vampires, and what do you get in return? Nothing. So don't waste your resources with these customers. Instead, spend your time finding another customer that will value what you do and will allow you to earn a profit on your goods or services.

6. It is not so smart to apply for credit from one bank at a time. Look, here's a fact: banks don't move at the speed of other businesses. If you think it will take a month to apply for a loan, be approved, and close on the loan, then count on it taking three months at least. And don't forget, they may even take two months before they tell you that were not approved. And you just lost valuable time banking on one bank to help you with your funding requirements. Here's a tip: If you need to borrow money, apply for loans with several banking institutions immediately. That way, you have more options of getting approved and you may even be able to get better rates and terms if you shop around. Be sure to let the different banks know you're doing that because as the tagline goes, "When banks compete, you win!" Don't forget that banks move slowly, and don't forget that as much as they may like you as a person, that won't help you get approval.

So don't be overly loyal to your banker-buddy because you have a fiduciary responsibility to fund your business and that trumps your buddy's commission check.

7. It is not so smart to apply for a loan only when you need the money. Have you noticed that banks don't like to lend money to people who need it? Well, that's a strong reason for you to apply for a line of credit with a bank before you ever need it. If you don't need the money today, you're much more likely to be approved than if you do need the money. So make sure you get funding when you don't need it (and then don't touch it unless and until you need it!).

8. It is not so smart to think your accountant is the best in the world. I used to have the best accountant in the world until I found out years later that he wasn't. He was a great guy, and he had sufficient abilities when we were a small company. But as our company grew, we eventually became too big for his abilities, and as a result, we eventually had to spend a ton of money getting our books straightened out by a different accountant. I was lucky in that the audit ended up showing we had overpaid in taxes instead of the other way around. But that money should have been in our bank account before the audit and we shouldn't have had to spend a fortune making things right. Now, I use an external audit every year or two, just to quality-check the work of my own accountant. My accountant

must be pretty good since he supports me doing that! You may want to consider doing this. In fact, it might be considered to be not so smart if you don't.

9. It is not so smart to take your attorney's word for it even if you don't understand it. News flash: Attorneys are flawed people just like you and me! In my early days of being a business owner, I never read the legalese stuff. I just counted on my attorney to translate everything for me. But then, I realized that the terms of some agreements were not as I thought they were. My attorneys made mistakes. So then, I started to read the legalese, and if I had a question on something's meaning, I asked for a translation. If the answer didn't satisfy me or if it didn't make sense to me, I questioned it. I even asked that it be rewritten in a way I could understand. At first, I was worried that my attorney may be offended by me being involved in the legal matters, but then it occurred to me that I really don't care if an attorney is offended by me wanting to do my job! If you're a business owner, it's your job to make sure you understand the content of documents you're asked to sign. Don't hide behind your attorney, you're the boss, and ultimately, you're holding the bag so you better get it right.

10. It is not so smart to hold people back. I've seen cases where people were held back because "we can't afford to lose him from the position he's

in." That's bull. If you hold people back from promotion opportunities or from moving to a new position inside or outside of your company, then you're making a big mistake. If you have a perfect candidate for a promotion but can't lose that person from being in the position they currently hold, then you have to own that problem. Don't make your people suffer. Instead, work your tail off to find a solution that will allow your deserving people to excel. If you do hold that person back, it's only a matter of time until you lose that person anyway.

11. It is not so smart to expose yourself to the dangers of being too safe. Sometimes, it's smart to play it safe by not exposing yourself to risks in business. But sometimes, the most dangerous thing you can do is to stay put and not take risks. There's an old saying that "You can't steal second base with your foot on first." If you're not content with the way things are then you have to do new things and new things generally involve risk. I've seen businesses cling to the past, afraid of change, afraid of dangers, and end up getting hammered as a result of being idle. Remember, too, that a lot of brilliant people with grand ideas never had the guts to pull the trigger and opportunity passed them by. I don't ever suggest you gamble your business on a single move, but I do suggest you allow yourself the opportunity to try new things.

12. It is not so smart to try to overly leverage yourself with too much debt. This sounds like advice for young people, but this bad move is made by young and old alike. I know all about this one because I've done it, more than once, mind you! I know, I know, we work hard, we deserve the fruits of our labor even before we can pay cash for it. But we want what we want and we think, "I can afford the monthly bill, so why not?" Most wealthy people will tell you that this isn't the way to achieve financial freedom and the peace of mind that comes with it. It's a good way to have a lot of nice things, but they're just that: things. Instead, make savings or investing a monthly bill. Commit to paying that bill on time every month and then do it. After you've paid your soul by investing in your future, then you'll know what other debt you can truly afford. If you don't know what I mean when I say "pay your soul," try making a monthly savings or investment a bill, pay it on time each month, and soon you'll know exactly what I mean.

13. It is not so smart to be rigid when flexibility may be called for. Discipline is great. Standards are necessary. Rules are good. But strong leaders occasionally exercise discretion instead of always staying hard and fast to things. When someone screws up and feels badly about it, you may want to consider giving them a pass and spare them the speech and the consequences. You'll be making a big deposit into that person's emotional bank

account and they'll remember it. If a time comes where a rule or process just doesn't make sense, remember that "function" trumps "form" almost every time. Don't be a square. Leave some room for flexibility or you'll be snapped like a stick for your rigidity and you'll alienate people that accept that we're all in this together.

14. It is not so smart to miss a funeral. You can skip a wedding if you don't feel like going, but don't miss a funeral or memorial service when one of your team member loses a loved one. Your being there and showing your support will never be forgotten and it's the right thing to do.

15. It is not so smart to miss an opportunity to make someone feel special. People don't care how much you know until they know how much you care. Enough said.

16. It is not so smart to rehire someone who burned you once already. I've never seen it work.

17. It is not so smart to be unethical. We all know that being dishonest or unethical is a sure way to ruin your reputation with other people, but that's not the biggest problem. The biggest problem is that you let down the person closest to you in your life: yourself. Don't take on that baggage.

18. It is not so smart to be too loyal to vendors. Loyalty is great, but as Ronald Reagan said, you have a responsibility to, "Trust, but verify." Otherwise, you may find that your vendors are taking your kindness and relationships for

granted and are rewarding you with higher prices and/or sacrificed service. I'm not suggesting that you avoid building strong relationships with your vendors. You absolutely should. But make sure you verify things once in a while by asking for competitive quotes and never allow your friends to slip in their service to your company.

19. It is not so smart to judge a person based on his worst day and equally as not so smart to judge a person on his best day. This is self-explanatory.

20. It is not so smart to allow your best performers to hold you hostage. I can't tell you how many times I've seen business owners figuratively held hostage by their super stars. Here's how it goes: The owner believes she needs the star performer. The star performer believes that too. But instead of having grace and appreciating the opportunity, the star feels entitled to do whatever he or she wants with no fear of repercussion. The owner is fearful of losing the person, so he or she puts up with the star's continuous destructive behavior. Sometimes, the star even builds a fiefdom around him or herself and "hijacks" the company. If you ever find yourself in that position, I have some advice that may help you a lot: Cut that person loose. You don't need that person as much as you think you do. In fact, once that person is gone, your entire company will get better and you'll find a replacement that is much more worthy to be on

your team. You'll likely find out that the super star wasn't nearly the star you thought he was.

21. It is not so smart to allow people to build fiefdoms in your company. See above.

22. It is not so smart to avoid responsibility when your company messes up. You will make mistakes. Your people will make mistakes. Someone will drop a ball and tick off a customer. I know this sounds odd, but mistakes have opportunities within them. When you directly and even dramatically own your mistakes instead of running from them or blaming someone else, you'll build huge credibility with your customers. People know that mistakes happen. They won't be happy about it at the moment, but when that moment passes, the way you responded to your mistake will long be remembered and appreciated.

23. It is not so smart to be sloppy with your financials. You have to have a complete understanding of what's going on in your business in order to know how you can improve it. Furthermore, bad financials equal bad (or nonexistent) tax returns and obviously, that's dangerous territory.

24. It is not so smart to miss an opportunity to celebrate with you team. When you celebrate the wins together, you build camaraderie. If you have a win and you don't take the time to celebrate and recognize it, then you're leaving a rewarding part of life out of your company and

missing a great opportunity to build a sense of pride and teamwork within your business.

25. It is not so smart to simply abdicate responsibility. Delegating is great, but never completely bury your head in the sand because ultimately, everything falls on the top leader in one way or another. The best leaders know this and accept it.

26. It is not so smart to borrow money from people you employ. That's bad form and everyone knows it. Don't do it under any circumstances.

27. It is not so smart to allow a bad relationship with a partner to affect your company. If you are in a partnership and the two of you don't get along, then you need to get help. Go see a business coach, a therapist, a mediator, a mutually trusted advisor or friend. Do what you need to do, but do not allow your team to know you have issues. I've seen companies (yes, more than one) where each of two partners actually had their own "following" of people. Can you imagine that? A divided company can't prosper and it's incredibly unhealthy for everyone. "Unity of command" is a must.

28. It is not so smart to allow things to fester instead of addressing things candidly. Some people rip into everyone for everything. Other people just let it bottle up inside of them. Both are bad ideas. Adults are supposed to be able to have constructive adult conversations with each other

in an adult way. But I understand that some people aren't receptive to criticism so taking the path of least resistance seems appealing. That's a ticking time bomb, so address your issues real time in a productive adult way and require your team to do the same.

29. It is not so smart to think that success is determined by how many people you employ. I'm guilty as charged! I used to love it when we hit milestones of employing people, such as 50 or 100. One day, I was bragging to one of our shareholders about how many people we employed. He responded by asking me if it were more important to me to have a huge payroll or more important to me to run the most efficient company I could. That question changed my perspective about hiring people and efficiency and profits improved as a result of that paradigm shift.

30. It is not so smart to break laws. And your mother told you that.

31. It is not so smart to allow anyone in your company to be picked on. If you allow this type of behavior, then you have major leadership issues. It's not funny, it's not healthy, it's not cute, and it's not cool.

32. It is not so smart to not keep your word. Everyone knows that. But sometimes people commit to things and then don't follow through. Generally, people don't break promises on purpose. They

simply forget about things. When you put something out there, make sure you deliver on your promises.

33. It is not so smart to think you're above the law. I'm not just talking about actual laws; I'm also talking about the "self-imposed laws" that are stated in your company's values statement. You have to lead by example and play by the same rules everyone else is expected to abide by.

34. It is not so smart to make any decision that could wipe out your company. I've seen it happen a few times. It's important to make decisions and try things that involve risk, but it's unwise to try things that will force your company into bankruptcy if they don't pan out. The most heart-breaking example of this I saw happened to a seventy-five-year-old employee-owned printing company. Desperate to increase sales, they bought a press that cost over a million dollars. It would open up new markets for them and solve their profitability and cash flow issues. Well, it didn't. Instead, it put them into bankruptcy and as a result, fifty people lost their jobs and their retirement savings.

35. It is not so smart to talk to people like they're stupid. Once you pierce a person's dignity, you've destroyed their trust and have blown any chance of having a good relationship with that person. Demoralizing people robs them of the confidence they need in order to be their best. If

making other people feel stupid makes you feel smarter and is a way of validating yourself, then go ahead and do it. But remember what Forest Gump said: "Stupid is as stupid does."

36. It is not so smart to think your people are there to serve you when in fact the truth should be just the opposite. The strongest type of leader in existence is the servant leader. There is nothing so powerful as service to others. When you make people feel safe and cared for, they will follow you. They'll serve each other, your company, your customers, and you with as much vigor as they can muster. But serving others must start with you, the leader.

37. It is not so smart to tell someone that you "told them so." It's not so smart to say that because they already know you told them so. And by making it about you, it becomes a pride issue instead of a learning point. Instead, ask them what they'll do differently next time and what lessons they learned. End by giving them your vote of confidence that this was a learning experience and that you're confident they'll do better next time. In other words, make it about them and make it about a learning point instead of making it about you being smarter than they are. When you say, "I told you so," you might as well say, "I'm insecure in myself and I got this one right, but you didn't listen and you're an idiot." Please don't be that person!

38. It is not so smart not to trust your gut! It's funny…we believe the things we see, hear, smell, touch, and taste, but what if your gut feelings were your sixth sense? Or what if your gut feelings were the sum of the other five senses? Too often, we ignore that feeling and regret it later!

A FINAL THOUGHT TO HELP YOU

You've just read about thirteen different strategies that could dramatically increase your company profits, significantly increase the value of your company, and help you realize the lifestyle you desired when you started your own business.

If this book made you smarter, then that's great. But being smarter doesn't automatically translate into being better. You have to do the work. The action steps you've been provided will guide you in getting things started, keeping things moving, and ultimately, in achieving your desired results.

Business ownership is not an event, it's a continual process that requires planning, execution of plans, measuring results, adjusting plans, and going back into executing those new adjusted plans.

The biggest challenges we face in our businesses (and in our personal lives) have nothing to do with a lack of knowledge. Instead, the biggest challenges are generally centered on a lack of focus, inspiration, accountability, discipline, energy, or any other state of mind that we allow to hold us back from doing the things we know we should be doing. In other words, we know what to do, we just don't always do what we know. And we pay dearly for that.

If you want some help in avoiding that trap, then I have a final tip for you: Hire a business coach.

The best athletes in the world have coaches. The best actors and actresses have coaches. Top CEOs and business executives have coaches. Why? Because coaching works!

Your business coach will keep you moving in a straight line toward reaching your goals and achieving your vision. When life happens, your coach will be there to help you get through rough spots. When things stabilize, your coach will refocus you on the major business initiatives that you were working on. It is his or her job to keep you aligned and focused on the things that are most important to you and to help you stay on track with your actions.

But not all business coaches are created equally. You have to find an expert business coach that knows business, understands business coaching fundamentals, and has access to additional resources to help you. Your coach does not need to know your particular industry, but he/she should be knowledgeable in sales, marketing, customer service, understanding the financials, leadership development, systems and systems implementation, strategic planning, personal effectiveness, human resources, and exit planning/succession planning.

Here are some additional tips when hiring a business coach:

If the coach isn't currently being coached him or herself, you may want to disqualify that person immediately. It's important that people practice what they preach.

Don't get caught up with razzle-dazzle. Choose the coach that you feel a connection with and who you enjoy being around. You'll invest a lot of time with your coach, so choose someone you like and respect.

Make sure that person understands business. There are a lot of coaches out there who are life coaches who choose to work with business owners. But they may or may not have the necessary business skills required to help you achieve your objectives. Ask coach-candidates about their own personal business experience and be sure you're comfortable that that person's talents and abilities are a match with what you're looking for.

Check references. Ask to speak with current clients and also former clients!

Ask what professional affiliations the coach-candidate is involved in and how that translates into a value for you.

Don't lock yourself into a long-term contract. Business transformation takes time and you should not expect quick fixes. So you should be committed to your coach relationship being an ongoing long-term commitment. That said, you have a fiduciary responsibility to your business and to yourself to make sure you have an "easy out" if you ever want to terminate the relationship. I would be concerned about the integrity or skill level of any person who felt a need to "lock me in" with a long-term contract without providing me an easy-out provision. A coaching relationship is important and valuable, but it should always be a mutually voluntary relationship.

When you hire a coach, take it seriously. You can have the best business coach on the planet, but if you aren't willing to live up to your end of the bargain, then it won't work. Conversely, if you're committed to change and are driven to get the results you've always wanted, hiring a business coach can make all the difference for you. Business coaching works extremely well, but a good coach won't carry you. You have to be committed to doing the work and leaving your comfort zone from time to time. Don't get me wrong: You're ultimately calling all the shots! A good coach won't bully you into doing anything you don't want to do. You should never agree to or execute a plan you don't personally support. But when you make a commitment with your coach to do something, you have to deliver. Good intentions alone are meaningless. You have to do the work. Your coach provides the benefit of clarity, focus, encouragement, different ideas or perspectives, and he or she will continually challenge you to be better at your job and in your life. But at the end of it all, the success of this relationship depends on your commitment to the process.

I wish you all my best! Go get unstuck.

—Jon

ABOUT THE AUTHOR

 Jon Denney is president and CEO of the Professional Business Coaches Alliance (PBCA) – North America's premier alliance of independent business coaches. Jon is the primary instructor at the PBCA Training Center in Syracuse, New York. Prior to becoming a professional business coach, Jon was the founder and CEO of digital printing businesses serving upstate New York markets. He has first-hand experience in all of the strategies in Unstuck! Jon has started companies, grown them, systematized them, built strong leadership teams, earned high profits, and has successfully sold and transitioned his companies which continue to operate profitably today (without him)!

Jon has four children (Kevin, Peyton, Oliver, and Jonna) and resides in Chittenango, New York.